An intelligent guide to

# REAL ESTATE DEVELOPMENT

## RON FORLEE

ISBN: 978-1-922409-73-7
Published by Vivid Publishing
A division of Fontaine Publishing Group
P.O. Box 948, Fremantle
Western Australia 6959
www.vividpublishing.com.au

A catalogue record for this
book is available from the
NATIONAL
LIBRARY    National Library of Australia
OF AUSTRALIA

# CONTENTS

# *ACKNOWLEDGMENTS*

This book would not have been possible without the support and encouragement of certain people. They have, in many ways, contributed to my life. I express my gratitude to:

My late mother Mabel, who supported and encouraged me to live my dreams but also taught me the importance to help less fortunate people.

My late wife, Cindy, who had always loved and supported me throughout our 38 years of marriage and showed me the importance of being happy and positive.

My children Taryn, Jared and Charisse who have loved and supported me in every possible way.

Ron Forlee

# THE AUTHOR

Ron is an architect, developer and author. He is also the Managing Director of AYR International Pty Ltd, an international real estate development advisory company and Archiplan Pty Ltd, an Australian based architectural practice.

Over the past 40 years, Ron has been involved in a range of real estate developments from housing estates, hotels to shopping centres which he has managed and financed. As an architect, he has master-planned large-scale communities and infrastructure projects and designed commercial buildings such as shopping centres, office blocks and tourism developments in Australia, South Africa and China.

By undertaking his own personal real estate developments, Ron has hands-on experience in real estate and infrastructure development. Being an expert in the field of real estate development, infrastructure, master planning and architecture, Ron has written and published several books on real estate development and on building construction. He has also delivered several papers at seminars about his pet interest.

In addition to book writing, Ron provides educational courses on real estate development through his website www.ronforlee.com. These courses are based on the culmination of over four decades as an Architect and Real Estate Developer. One of the motivating reasons for providing these mentorship programs is to educate people to undertake developments for the right purpose. Developers should make money as they are taking a significant risk, but this should not be the sole motivating factor. Developers are decision-makers in creating environments for our future generations. So it is, therefore, their responsibility to create environments that are ecologically sustainable that can be enjoyed by all.

# *PREFACE*

In 2004 I published my first book, *An Intelligent Guide to Australian Property Development* followed by *Australian Residential Property Development* in 2005. In 2014, due to the overwhelming interest, I wrote *Australian Residential Property Development for Investors*. I recently published *Fast Track to Passive Income* for developer and investors.

The first two books are now out of print. Due to the keen interest from a new generation of young developers, I decided to re-publish and update the content of these two books. This book *"An Intelligent Guide to Real Estate Development"* provides a good overview of real estate development. It is not a technical book and has been written not only for the novice developer, but to seasoned developers as well. It aims to offer a sound approach to and defines the risks involved in real estate development so that you do not become another sad financial statistic. While this book has been written within the Australian context, many of the development principles apply to other countries.

In the early stages of my architectural career, I became interested in real estate development. Architecture is creative in nature, and architects are continually exploring new building ideas and concepts. Real estate development has allowed them to test these ideas. In my pursuit for knowledge on this subject, I have searched and read many books on real estate investment. During this period, I found that most books available concentrated on existing residential real estate investment, and very few covered the area of development. The few books that have been written on this subject are highly technical and theoretical in nature and are not written in layman's language. What I also found was that most of these real estate investment books provide content are on how much money the authors made in their real estate transactions but did not point out the real pitfalls that exist.

Any person contemplating entering real estate development will be overwhelmed by the incredible breadth and depth of knowledge required to make it a success. No development should be made without understanding areas such as law, finance, management, feasibilities, tax, company structures and marketing. From the first chapter to the last, I cover a broad range of subjects. The subjects covered include whether you have the right attitude, development finance, feasibility studies, the timing of a project and the appointment of consultants. Also, it shows you how to analyse profits and provides advice on a range of development projects from small residential to large commercial centres.

Having experienced both success and failure in my 40 years as a real estate developer, I have learnt a great deal, especially from my mistakes. It is because of these experiences and from advising many clients on their projects that I can write this book and give practical guidance on this exciting but risky industry. In essence, I wish I had this book available before the start of my career. I hope that you will find it useful and that you will benefit from the subjects covered.

Ron Forlee B. Arch
Email: ron@ayrinternational.com
June 2020

# Chapter 1

# *INTRODUCTION*

Why do people develop real estate? Unless they are a government organisation, the obvious answer is money and success. The astute have made significant profits from real estate investments that provides them with ongoing income and capital growth. Every developer has his or her own financial goals. These are dependent on several variables such as income, age, taxation levels and social status, but the underlying motivation to develop real estate remains the same — success and wealth.

In the area of real estate, developments can be ranked as the most exhilarating and satisfying if approached positively and with the full understanding of the risk involved. Globally, with increasing population and urbanisation, there are an incredible amount of opportunities for the eager developer, be it land development, speculative renovation, residential or commercial projects. We often hear of individuals who have made tremendous financial gains from their developments. Still, and unfortunately, there are equal numbers that have been unsuccessful.

There is an element of risk attached to almost every significant financial reward; however, with real estate development, the risks can be calculated and analysed. Not all developers have the same set of priorities and as such focus their efforts in different areas. Some concentrate on residential buildings, while others become shopping centre specialists where the projects are larger with more significant returns.

If you are contemplating entering the real estate industry as a developer or investor, you will be overwhelmed by the incredible amount of knowledge required to be successful. Besides understanding areas such as law, finance, management, feasibilities, tax, company structures and marketing, there are the various asset classes under both residential and commercial real estate to be learnt as well. This book provides a good overview of real estate development and a foray into the industry. However, one must study each subject in more detail and most importantly is gain practical experience.

To call yourself a developer, one does not need a degree or higher level of education and nor carry a license. Unlike a doctor or architect, university education and registration with an institute are required to practice. It is an interesting dilemma, as developers are the creators and decision-makers of the urban fabric for our current and future communities. Therefore, the underlying message is that a career in real estate development can reap handsome profits in line with the risks undertaken. However, in doing so, developers should act responsibly and create developments that are sustainable both environmentally and operationally, not only for the present but for future generations as well.

# Chapter 2

# WHY REAL ESTATE DEVELOPMENT?

## Introduction

Any change to the existing use of land can be defined as real estate development. It can be a small land rezoning and sub-division to a multi-storey office block. The category of real estate development is broad and each category, although similar in principle, must be tackled differently. For example, the development of an office block is influenced by the vacancy rate of the time. In contrast, a shopping centre development is determined by the demand of the surrounding demographics.

## High risk, high profits

Many financial institutions regard real estate development as a high-risk area but, as the adage goes, 'the higher the risk, the higher the reward'. People usually develop a real estate with the specific aim of profiting from significant capital gains. Capital gain is the difference between the initial purchase price and selling price in the sale of an asset minus costs, or the actual profit made. If you intend to enter this business, it is best to start small and learn from your experience without losing any money. It means that starting in the residential arena would be a safer bet than venturing into a commercial or industrial development where higher expertise and financial commitment are required.

## Rewards in real estate development

Every business or investment has specific qualitative attributes that will make it appealing to certain people. Real estate development as a business or investment is no different, and it can offer the following benefits:

## Leverage potential

Generally, most developments are made with the use of borrowed funds, otherwise known as "leveraging". It means that the larger percentage of the capital cost of the development is borrowed debt with a small amount of personal equity which realises a significant return than the initial money invested. The simple Table 1.1 below shows this:

| | Property 1 (unleveraged) | Property 2 (leveraged) |
|---|---|---|
| Total development cost | $1,200,000 | $1,200,000 |
| Mortgage funds (debt) | nil | $800,000 |
| Personal equity | $1,200,000 | $400,000 |
| Net profit (assume 20%) | $ 240,000 | $240,000 |
| Less interest (5% pa spread) | nil | $ 60,000 |
| Gross profit | $ 240,000 | $180,000 |
| % on equity invested | 20% | 45% |

TABLE 1.1: Unleveraged versus leveraged

## Tax benefits

There are several tax incentives for the private sector to invest in real estate development, which also assists the various housing and infrastructure needs of our increasing population. These laws provide for:

- The deduction of expenses associated with the development.
- The deduction of interest charges.
- The deduction to any real estate taxes related to the development.
- The deduction of most depreciating items.
- Capital gains tax relative to inflation.
- Negative gearing opportunities.

Tax benefits will vary according to the development vehicle (e.g. company, trust etc). Before establishing a development vehicle, obtain advice from a qualified accountant. As most developments involve large sums of money, most developers are registered GST vendors. It allows them to claim the GST for goods and services but must charge a GST when they sell the development to a third party.

## Entrepreneurial opportunities

Compared to other investments such as shares, real estate development can offer several entrepreneurial business opportunities. Through your own labour and limited capital input, you can make a vision come to fruition (and pocket a healthy profit) by improving or renovating existing buildings or rezoning and subdividing land. Many real estate millionaires started with small scale residential or renovation developments. Today these entrepreneurs are building our cities and creating job opportunities.

## Creative financing

Yields and profits from real estate development can be significantly improved by creative financing techniques and smart negotiating strategies. Astute developers, with a thorough understanding of how to finance new projects, have started developments with minimal personal financial outlay. Some creative developers I know of have managed to secure 100 per cent financing without any security except the property being developed.

## Equity build-up

If you decide to retain your development as a long-term investment, your monthly principle repayments, and the increase in inflationary capital gain is continually increasing the value of your equity. This equity can be used to provide for a deposit for another development or sold and leveraged for a larger project.

## Increasing market

With the constant increase in population, there is a continuous demand for new shelter and infrastructure needs. In every new residential suburb development, there are ancillary needs such as schools, shopping centres, medical centres and so on. Besides, there are thousands of real estate sales consultants and brokers advocating the qualities of real estate as an investment. The effect of these beliefs and claims provide a continuous flow of buyers and help to improve real estate prices.

## Risk in real estate development

Despite the positive aspects of real estate development, there will always be risks involved. The stakes are high, and if caution is not taken, you could lose not only your capital but also some or all of your assets as well as the loss of sleep and peace of mind. Risks that may be encountered are:

### Bad purchases

Developers always face the risk of either paying too much for a property or buying in the wrong location. It can happen if the developer is impatient and does not undertake due diligence or gathering the correct market information. Alternatively, the developer is influenced by an overzealous real estate sales consultant. The risk of a bad purchase can be reduced by better-negotiating skills and more extensive market research.

### Business failure

All forms of business run the risk of failure, and the business of real estate development is no exception. It can occur as a result of bad management, a decline in the local economy, change in consumer tastes or even bad timing. Proper management, careful market research and creative marketing can help reduce the likelihood of this type of failure.

### Reduced liquidity

Real estate is not a commodity that can be easily traded on a day-to-day basis, like shares on the stock exchange. Developments take a great deal of time in planning and marketing before there is a transfer of cash and there is always the possibility of being forced to hold the property for a lengthy period when the market is down.

## Market-specific

A new development concept or trend may be very successful in a specific city or country. Still, it may be a complete failure in another. A planning concept may take time to be accepted by a new market as traditions and trends vary from locality to locality. By the time consumer interest is shown, the developer may have lost a considerable amount of capital. Thorough market research and smart planning to the local market needs will help to alleviate this risk.

## Changes to laws and regulations

Any changes to government laws or local authority regulations under the present systems can alter the expected returns from a development project. Also, real estate developments are subjected to several laws. These include both state and local government laws such as environmental protection acts and new building by-laws, amongst others. Careful attention to any possible changes in political and social movements can help the developer to plan strategies around these changes.

## Holding period

Most buyers of new developments do so with borrowed funds or buy conditional upon the sale of an existing property. This process can take a considerable amount of time before the sold property is settled. In the interim, the developer is left holding the property, forcing him to pay interest on the money borrowed.

Alternatively, a development may not be able to be built in phases. It may have to be completed in a single phase such as with an apartment block. The holding period could cost the developer a considerable amount of funds if only half the development is sold. Allowing for this factor in your feasibility study and excellent negotiating skills will help to alleviate any losses incurred during a holding period.

## Conclusion

Real estate development is not a simple business and nor is it for the faint-hearted. Venturing into this industry will require the developer's full attention. There are no short cuts, and there is a considerable knowledge to be gained and information gathered before one can make a valued judgement on a development project. However, if you work hard at it, you can reap significant financial rewards.

# Chapter 3

# THE ATTRIBUTES OF SUCCESSFUL DEVELOPERS

## Introduction

Successful real estate developers are not created overnight. Their success is a culmination of education, attitude, experience, instinct and seeking the right advice. With the constant changes in the real estate industry, individuals in this business must monitor and be aware of these changes. They must be one step ahead so that they can either take advantages of new opportunities or to alter their strategies to avoid risk. For example, seasoned developers who sold their developments at the peak of the boom will be taking advantage of the next downturn. They will be purchasing cheaper land for their future projects. If you want to tackle the development world, you must have strong financial backing, a good understanding of the market, a hunger for knowledge and a strong level of commitment.

## Do you have the right attributes?

Before venturing into the development game, be honest and ask yourself the following questions:

- Do you have the knowledge or experience to tackle a development project?
- Can you afford the time away from your regular job to manage the building?

As well, look at the following principles and see if you feel comfortable in pursuing them.

## Know your limitations

As real estate development can be broken into several categories, it is essential before you embark on a specific project, that you should know your limitations. These include, amongst others, your financial resources, your knowledge of the type of development, your network of advisers and your understanding of the local conditions. Also, do you have the drive and motivation to see the project from start to finish? Do you have a passion for small detail? If you have another job, can you afford the time to manage your project? By careful planning and visualising your end product, you will reap the rewards of your endeavours.

## Be realistic

We often hear of motivational speakers endorsing the principle of "think big". While this may be a bold outlook, you still have to be realistic about the possible pitfalls and the economic environment. Donald Trump, one of the most recognised developers in the modern era, has recognised this and believes in thinking big. He believes that most people think small because most people are afraid of success and winning. Most of Donald Trump's developments are in America (where everything is big). America has a large population that naturally creates a strong market force, so he can afford the luxury of thinking big. If you want to think big, think big within the parameters of your market and your capabilities. If your big idea fits the right conditions, then you have to remain focused to the point that you become obsessive and passionate about your project.

## Become an expert

To become an outstanding developer, you must become an expert. To achieve this status, you have to educate yourself by obtaining as much knowledge as possible about the industry. It does not necessarily mean that you have to go back to school and spend several years studying. An alternative method is to read various books related to real estate development and investment. Read real estate articles, listen to blogs, attend seminars, join local industry associations and learn to network with people within real estate circles. Also, ask questions from experts and professionals in the industry, but most of all, learn from your own experience. Knowledge is power, and with this power, you will be able to make informed decisions and reduce the risk in whatever project you are about to tackle.

### Take care of the pitfalls.

When it comes to real estate development, there is no such thing as gambling; instead, you can consider it more 'calculated' gambling. It means that every decision you make is analysed before the 'go-ahead' is given. Motivational speakers state that to be successful in anything you do, you must think positively. While this is the correct approach, you must be still conservative and look at the negative aspects. By planning for the pitfalls, you will be ready to avoid them. If you have a good idea, take a sheet of paper and draw a vertical line down the centre. On the right side, list all the negative aspects and on the left, all the positive. If the positives outnumber the negatives, then you should be confident in moving ahead. Naturally, the negative elements will need to be worked on before you go too much further.

### Maximise your options

Real estate development is a risky business, and to protect oneself, one must be flexible. Never get emotionally attached to a specific development you are undertaking. Be prepared to walk away from a project if you feel that things are not working in your favour, especially from a business point of view. It is easy to fall into the emotional trap if you have spent a considerable amount of time and effort in developing a concept to a point where it becomes an obsession. By maximising your options, you will arrive with at least five options to make the opportunity work. Remember that anything can change, even to the best-laid plans.

### Know your market

Some people have an intuitive feel for the market, and some have no idea at all. Some people say that you must be born with an instinct or feel for the real estate market. Many success stories, such as Bill Gates and Warren Buffet, to name a few, have an intuitive feel for their respective fields. For a developer, the real estate game is not much different. For those of us who were not blessed with such insight, it is essential to read about and keep up with market trends. Undertaking market surveys is one way of doing this but be aware that they are not always 100 per cent correct and are also expensive. Another way to analyse your market is to ask everyone (including your friends, financial adviser and colleagues), for their opinions before you decide. For example, if you are contemplating developing a particular piece of property, ask the people in the surrounding area what they think of issues such as the local schooling, shops, transport and crime.

## Be persistent

If you have a good idea and a strong belief that you will succeed but encounter obstacles such as a lack of finance or a council's disapproval, fight back or strategise around the problem. Confrontation is not always the best approach, as it often alienates people, which may delay your plans. A better way is to think laterally and work out strategies so that everybody (or nearly everybody) wins in the end. Some developers believe that if they cannot obtain their approval for a project within a specific timeframe, they may have missed the market opportunity and may as well abandon the project. If you cannot find a solution to satisfy all parties within a reasonable timeframe, walk away and look for a new opportunity. There is always another one around the corner.

## Build a good reputation

The building industry is riddled with stories of bad workmanship and poor service. And we often hear of developers promoting and selling inferior products. Remember the old adage: you can fool some of the people some of the time, but not all of the people all of the time. It is easy to spend a great deal of money on marketing your development. Still, if you do not deliver the goods as promised, people will eventually catch on, and you may lose more money in the long term.

If you want to make money out of this business, there are no short cuts. Attention to detail is a prerequisite to success in this industry. Like any other successful business, superior quality service is of utmost importance. Remember that in most instances, the customer is right. It is best to fix a problem immediately before it festers and gets out of hand. It will enhance your reputation as a credible and trustworthy developer.

## Watch the pennies

As the proverb says, "save the pennies and the pounds will look after themselves". It is a precondition in any development undertaken. We often hear of projects blowing the budget and leading to failure. Spend where it is necessary to sell your development, but don't spend unnecessarily, and primarily not just to satisfy your ego. Learn to be cost-conscious and never throw money around. Be strict with your financial control and always get at least three prices, compare them and, most importantly, get it in writing. Treat all your consultants and contractors fairly. If they deliver the goods or services on time, pay them on time, but if they do not keep to their promises or overcharge you, get on the phone immediately and complain.

## Selecting the type of development

Before deciding on the type of development, you want to tackle, carefully review the market conditions, your own business experience and your financial resources. Although this book is written for the novice developer who may only want to develop a small speculative home or small commercial development, the following list outlines various types of developments that may also interest a seasoned developer.

### Types of Developments

The list below is a brief explanation of the various types of developments.

*Residential*

The residential category of real estate development is where most developers cut their teeth. It can include a single-family residence (either speculative or renovated for resale), unit, duplex, triplex and quadruplex, as well as more extensive strata unit developments such as townhouses, villas and retirement villages.

### Apartments

Apartments are also known as flats or condominiums. Developments in this category can range from simple double-storey units to multistorey, mixed-use buildings.

### Commercial offices

Commercial office buildings can vary in size and quality according to finishes (which include wall and floor tiles, carpets and partitions). They can be renovated homes, strata-titled, high-rise structures or low-rise business parks.

### Retail

The retail category includes the small corner shop, strata-titled showrooms, neighbourhood shopping centres, community centres and regional retail centres.

### Industrial

Industrial buildings are simple in design, providing large, open spaces for manufacturing or storage. These developments can vary from light industrial (which include buildings for warehousing and small manufacturers) to heavy industrial (which are generally planned away from residential areas. A Petro-chemical plant is an example of this type of development).

### Land

The land category can include a subdivision of raw agricultural land or a subdivision of an older property. The demand for new land is created by the changes in urban planning due to population growth.

### Accommodation

Accommodation includes motels, hotels and holiday apartments that are generally located near holiday resorts that cater for temporary accommodation.

### Recreational

The recreational category can include entertainment centres, casinos, golf courses, sports stadiums and waterfront developments.

They can either stand-alone or be part of a mixed-use complex, together with retail outlets.

*Special purpose*

Other developments can include speciality buildings such as medical and childcare centres, theatres, research centres and other special-purpose buildings.

Table 3.1 (below) summarises the characteristics of the various types of developments.

| Development | Risk level | Financing | Expertise | Saleability |
|---|---|---|---|---|
| Single home | Low | Very good | Low | Good |
| Units | Low | Good | Medium | Good |
| Apartments | Medium | Average/good | Medium/high | Average/good |
| Land | Medium/high | Average/difficult | Medium/high | Depends on use |
| Accommodation | Medium/high | Average/difficult | High | Good/average |
| Offices | Medium/high | Good/average | Medium | Good/average |
| Retail | Medium/high | Good/average | Medium/high | Average |
| Industrial | Medium/high | Good/average | Medium | Good/average |
| Recreational | High | Difficult | High | Difficult |

TABLE 3.1: Development selection

## Size of development

The size of the development project will be dependent upon your financial resources. Although mortgage financing will allow you to leverage to more significant developments, one has to be careful and not "over gear" your equity position by borrowing too much debt. If your resources are limited, start with a smaller development. As you become more experienced, you can start reducing your equity contribution by using creative financing and intelligent negotiation.

## Location

If you are a first-time developer, try to look for development opportunities close to where you live or work. It will help you to know and understand the local market a lot better. You will be able to visit the property more frequently, therefore, keeping your building contractors under control. As you become more experienced and understand the broader market, you may decide to look at other areas where you can find more profitable opportunities.

## Return on development

Because the return on your investment (ROI) is one of the main motivating factors in developing real estate, it is the most critical aspect to consider when deciding whether the project should proceed. The development profit will vary from project to project and should be evaluated according to the risks being taken. You should also investigate the sort of returns other investments are making before settling on a course of action.

## Rent or sell?

Whether you rent or sell your finished development will depend upon your overall development and investment strategy. Many developers will build and sell, whereas others may want to own the buildings and build up their real estate portfolio. Your tax position should influence your decision to rent or sell, and your accountant would be the best person to advise you on this.

## Personal time

If you are presently employed or have a business that is not in the field of the building or allied to the development industry, make sure that you have the necessary time to manage and super-vise your project. Alternatively, employ a development or project manager to look after your interests. It is not wise to have two jobs at once as one of them will fail.

## Active or passive developer?

As a passive developer, you can become part of a real estate syndicate or invest in a development company that already has management in place to oversee its various projects. It is an ef-fective way to introduce yourself to the development game, as you will be able to learn a great deal about the industry before you venture out on your own. The passive developer does not own the property in his or her name but, instead, has an interest in an entity or a fund which, in turn, develops real estate. These can include:

## Limited partnerships

It could be a small partnership between two friends or larger syndication consisting of a group of businesspeople or investors who will appoint individual members of the group to run the operation. Today most partnerships form limited liability companies, appointing directors to run the operation.

## Property trust

These are unlisted or listed property trusts, under the management of development and financial experts. An unlisted trust is generally private, whereas the listed trust is listed on the stock exchange.

As an active developer, you would want to be involved in the day-to-day activities and management decisions. The decision of whether to have partners in the development, the level of expertise in management and marketing, the amount of finance required, and the amount of time available will influence the developer. Most active developers, especially in the residential sector, develop to sell. It is a full–time activity, whereas most passive developers hold their projects as long-term investments.

# Types of developers

As noted earlier, there are many different categories of developments. At the same time, there are different types of real estate developers. Developers can be defined in the following categories:

## Government and institutional developers

This category consists mainly of state governments and at times assisted by the Federal Government. Type of developments would be government offices, hospitals, police stations, industrial land sub-division and any other public institution. In some State-run programs they may involve the private sector, and either look at a joint venture or tender a developable portion of land to private developers.

### Corporate developers

This group includes real estate development companies and major financial institutions. They could be privately owned corporations, public companies listed on the Australian Stock Exchange, large insurance groups, superannuation funds or trade unions. Generally, these groups develop more significant commercial properties such as regional shopping centres intending to generate profits for their shareholders through long-term capital gain and good cash flow through positive rental income.

### Speculative developers

These developers undertake a development project intending to build and sell for the maximum profit. In the residential sector, they will build home units or apartments and market their product to the general public. At the same time, those involved in commercial projects would package development and sell the completed project to an institutional investor. Developers that fall under this category are mainly residential developers.

### Investor developers

Investor developers will undertake a project with a commitment from a few or even no tenants. They develop buildings intending to own and secure a long-term annual income stream together with an appreciation in the value of the property, therefore, increasing their equity. Some significant developers listed on the stock exchange specialise in developing shopping centres and office blocks as long-term investments.

### Renovator developers

These developers choose to buy an existing property and improve the value through cosmetic renovations and alterations or by converting its current use to a more viable form of real estate. There are many stories in magazines which provide examples of successful developers that fall under this category.

## Fee developers

Experienced developers may at times contract to develop another person's property in return for a set fee or a share into the development. As they are giving professional advice, they fully understand all phases of real estate development and minimise the risk on a project. As a real estate development manager, I have managed many successful projects on behalf investors for a set fee.

## Land developers

Land developers are mostly speculative developers but specialise in land development only. They develop parcels of land by rezoning, sub-dividing and provide the necessary infrastructure. When completed, they sell portions of the land to other developers or end-users. Some of these developers form syndications for purchasing large tracts of land, obtain all planning approvals and provide all the necessary infrastructure.

# Development ownership entities

Before starting your development, it is worthwhile spending some time with your accountant and determine which is the best vehicle to use as the owner of the development entity. Listed below are various types of ownership:

## Sole proprietor

Sole proprietary is the simplest form of ownership. You have total control of the development and are the sole decision-maker. This type of ownership can be used if you decide to hold on to your development as an investment and negative gear your tax position. To negative gear, one borrows funds to purchase an investment, and the repayments and interest on the loan exceed the income from your asset. The difference can be claimed as a tax deduction.

## Partnership

In a general partnership, two or more persons have ownership of a development business. All partners are personally responsible for management decisions taken and are liable for any debts incurred. The transfer of a general partnership interest usually results in the dissolution of the partnership.

### Limited liability company

Limited liability companies are made up of one or more share-holders with directors appointed from the shareholders to run the company. Profits and losses are passed on to the shareholders and with limited liability for its shareholders. The directors of the company are liable for the management of the company. They are not protected by limited liability. All limited liability companies are subject to the Australian Securities and Investment Commission (ASIC) rules and regulations.

### Public limited company

The public limited company is similar to the limited liability company, except this vehicle is offers to the general public smaller investment sizes or shares. Public shareholders must pay for their shares upon purchase. These companies are not allowed to borrow additional funds without the consent of the public shareholders.

### Joint venture

Joint ventures are used in place of a general partnership and are limited to a defined development. In most cases, joint ventures are formed where one party contributes the finance or equity, and the other party contributes to the land or development expertise.

### Trust

A trust is used as a basis for indirectly controlling a development company or a specific property, while still having access to the economic benefits of ownership. In a trust, one person (known as the trustee) is entrusted to hold, control or manage a property to the benefit of another (the beneficiary).

## Conclusion

If you feel that you have the right ingredients to be a successful developer, remember that there are no short cuts. It involves a great deal of time and do your homework. It means setting goals, learning the basics of real estate development, knowing the real estate cycles and networking with people in the industry.

Many would-be developers have failed because they have made decisions on too little information and little market research. These poor decisions can lead to paying too much for the property to be developed, unnecessary budgeting, under-pricing the development cost, and making unrealistic profit projections. Therefore not raising enough working capital to sustain the cash-flow of the project.

All decisions involving real estate development should be made on purely economic and business considerations - not based on emotion. During the process of your development, always investigate all aspects and make decisions on sound business practice. If you are uncertain about any issue, seek professional advice and do not make assumptions.

# Chapter 4

# DEVELOPING VERSUS INVESTING

## Introduction

Many books have been written about the benefits of investing in established properties, but what about developing your own investment properties? In general, with established real estate, wealth is created through capital appreciation over an extended period. This capital growth can take between five to ten years, where the growth in value plus your equity can increase at least in line with inflation. Instead of waiting for this capital to grow over time, there is a quicker process in improving your equity position, and that is through development. So, what are the advantages and will it benefit you financially? The decision for most people will depend predominantly on personal choice. Still, it could involve several other factors such as the availability of your time, personal financial situation, timing and location. The advantages and disadvantages of these two options are analysed below.

## Advantages of developing

There are several advantages to developing real estate.

### Free equity

If you have done your research and are a good negotiator, there is always an opportunity to purchase land and negotiate a building contract at discounted rates. If you are an experienced developer, you can save money by undertaking part of the project yourself. In each situation, you are creating 'free' or 'sweat' equity. It is the difference in value between the total development cost which includes land of the land and building costs, against market value of the completed development. For example, if the total capital cost for your development is $1 000 000 and the valuation after the project is $1 200 000, your free equity is $200 000.

## Design to suit the market trends

Depending on the age of the building, some investment properties may be too old or will outlive the market needs, in terms of accommodation and architectural style. For example, in a housing project, the rooms may be too small, the kitchen may look tired and not well planned, and the colours of the bathrooms may be over the top. Only with substantial cost and alterations can an older building be brought up to date with the latest trends. With new developments, however, you can plan and design the building to suit new market trends.

## Excitement of building

Watching your development plans as the architect or designer presents your design, selecting your finishes and watching the various stages of construction can be exhilarating and stimulating. When the public is overwhelmingly receptive to your product, and your development is quickly sold or leased, it can also be very satisfying. The same cannot be said of purchasing an established building. The excitement is limited, and there is always the possibility of renovating or adding new rooms to suit the market will be required.

## Longer life span

All older buildings have a certain amount of wear and tear and will require maintenance. Before buying an older building, engage the services of a building consultant to examine and uncover any structural defects, electrical faults, roof leaks and other potential problems. A younger building constructed to quality standards is less likely to require maintenance over a short period.

## Tax benefits

The depreciation allowance mentioned earlier is the proportion of the cost or the book value of a building, which may be deducted annually as a legitimate expense. It is usually determined by the original cost of the building set against the life of the building. The allowance, at the time of writing, is 2.5 per cent per annum over forty years. As a developer of a new project, you will receive the benefit of the full forty years.

### Less up-front capital required

Most real estate transactions that are financed require a deposit or similar equity, generally around 20 per cent. With new developments, the deposit is mainly needed when purchasing the land, which is lower in price than an established building that includes both the land and buildings. For example, if you bought an investment building at a market value of $1 000 000, you will require $200 000 cash or equity. With a development property in the same area developed at the cost of $800 000, you will need a $160 000 capital injection. Besides, there are incidental costs, such as stamp duty and conveyancing fees, which are generally higher in established real estate investment.

## Disadvantages of developing

There are several disadvantages in undertaking real estate development compared with investing in established properties.

### Budget blow-outs

When a completed building is offered for sale, buyers are usually aware of the bottom-line price that the seller is prepared to accept. It gives a certain degree of comfort to the investor, as the only additional costs include stamp duty and conveyancing fees. When developing a new property, developers know the fixed price of the land. Still, they can find themselves in a situation where the final cost of the building has blown out beyond their set budget. With a new building, there are many additional costs, such as landscaping, fencing, floor coverings, curtains and so on, that a builder does not usually include in the quoted price. Also, it is possible to get carried away and overcapitalise on the building. So that when it comes to selling, it is difficult to find a buyer to match the amount of money spent on the building.

### Inability to see what is being purchased

Unless you are building a replica of another building, most new buildings are developed from an idea or a concept and then into a set of working plans. To most people, reading and visualising the completed building from architectural drawings is a difficult task. Whereas, with an established building, you can walk through and obtain a feel of the layout and see the exact size of the rooms.

### Disputes with contractors

'Dodgy' builders are always making media headlines, which highlight unscrupulous practices and create a degree of scepticism about the building industry. Disputes with builders could delay the completion of the project, which increases the holding cost, thus reducing profit. These reports are enough to make most people shy away from tackling new developments. Fortunately, however, not all builders are dishonest, and most have a well-established reputation for quality work and excellent client relationships.

### Immediate return

When you invest in an established property, especially if it has a tenant with a long lease, you will be able to assess the value of your return immediately. On the other hand, when you develop a new property, the value of your return can only be evaluated when the building or buildings are completed and fully leased. It could take several months to a year or more.

## The comparison

Let us now compare the two hypothetical cases from a financial point of view. The example shown below is a three-unit housing development versus a group of three units on a single site that is five years old in the same location. The development has an assumed completed value at $1 500 000 like the existing property.

| New Development | | Established Development | |
|---|---|---|---|
| Land | $450,000 | 3 Housing Units | $1,500,000 |
| Stamp duty | $21,500 | Stamp Duty | $70,500 |
| Settlement cost | $3,500 | Purchasing Cost | $11,500 |
| Construction cost | $650,000 | | |
| Miscellaneous cost | $125,000 | | |
| Total development cost | $1,250,000 | Total purchase coat | $1,582,000 |
| 30% Equity Required | $375,000 | 30% Deposit Required | $450,000 |
| Increased equity on completion | $250,000 | Increased equity 1 year (CPI) | $37,500 |
| Revised equity | $625,000 | Revised equity | $487,500 |

From the above analysis, one can see that there is an opportunity where one can create "tax-free" increased equity, which can be used as a deposit for future investments. Please note that tax is payable on the profit if the development is sold on completion.

### The Decision

The financial decision whether to invest in a completed building or to develop your own will be based on a personal choice, and the factors pointed out above. There is nothing to beat the excitement and stimulation of new developments. Especially if you are prepared to negotiate land deals, work on the design with your architect or designer, selecting and negotiating with a builder and go through a certain amount of annoyance during construction.

## Residential versus commercial developments

In comparing the above, it is worthwhile comparing residential versus commercial developments and which offers better value. Residential is a lot easier to understand and to start with, while commercial requires more experience, which is associated with greater returns and higher risks. The critical difference between residential and commercial developments in the assessment of their value as an asset in dollar terms, as explained below:

- With residential, the value is based mainly on supply and demand in a specific location.
- With commercial, the value is based on the rental income (yield) of a building and what an investor buyer would reasonably pay to achieve that income or yield. For example, if an accepted yield for building in a specific is 5 per cent say $500 000, then the value of the building is $10 000 000.

Other differences between these assets are described below.

## Market research

In analysing the market for potential developments: Commercial real estate requires more intensive market research on a macro level whereas with residential, the supply and demand are localised.

## Long-term values

The long-term value of any property is based on variable factors, such as the neighbourhood, demographics, communal facilities, schools, transport and the local economy. Residential real estate in the right location allows for the most effective management and control of these variables. In contrast, commercial real estate can depreciate, for example, such as the closure of a road. Still, they can also have a monopoly if no further development is allowed which would create competition.

## Value-adding

Developers in residential real estate have the potential to add value of their properties by way of constructing another room or by renovating the kitchen. With commercial real estate, these opportunities are relatively limited, where local government regulations can prohibit large-scale renovation works. Still, on the positive side, the value can improve by undertaking cosmetic changes or change the lease on more favourable terms.

## Rental growth

Commercial real estate offers more significant opportunities for rental growth compared with residential. The rental yields are generally lower in residential properties. With commercial leases, the annual rental increases are usually in line with the Consumer Price Index (CPI) or by 4%, whereas this is not always achievable with residential real estate. Commercial real estate leases tend to be much longer from 3 to 10 years or more and are often secured by bank guarantees, which make them a secure investment.

## Market size

Residential real estate can cater to a broader market when compared to the sale of a commercial real estate. It is also easier to market and sell a residential development as it can be broken down into smaller units. Buildings such as an apartment block can be divided into strata sections and sold to several purchasers. Whereas, a commercial building with a similar floor area would look to a single purchaser.

## Initial investment

Most residential projects require a smaller amount of capital to get started compared with commercial. Also, lending institutions have the infrastructure and systems to make home loans more accessible for the consumer to apply for a loan. As commercial developments require substantial capital, the application for funding is more complex and would take longer in obtaining approval.

## Liquidity

With residential, finance is more readily available for end purchasers, making residential developments are a lot easier to sell than commercial developments. It allows the residential developer to exit his or her development earlier. With commercial developments, finding an end-buyer can be complicated as buyers are more sophisticated and will impose stringent conditions. Besides a commercial project will generally take longer to construct, therefore delaying the potential rental income.

## Purchasers

Purchasers of residential real estate are not as sophisticated compared to a seasoned investor interested in commercial properties. Commercial real estate investors will generally prolong negotiations that could delay the settlement. An offer on a residential property is usually completed on a standard offer and acceptance contract executed by a real estate agent. In contrast, with larger commercial properties, a solicitor would be required to formalise the purchase.

## Capital growth

During the boom period of a real estate cycle, residential properties have a far higher capital growth than commercial. A shortage of residential properties on the market will drive prices up. Whereas with commercial properties, their value is tied up to the term of a lease with only CPI annual escalation increasing its value. However, some commercial leases have a rent review over an agreed period to match the current market ren which makes up the loss of capital growth during the boom period.

## Leasing

Commercial properties can be harder to lease due to the specific requirements of commercial tenants. In some instances, owners who are pressed to find a commercial tenant will offer generous lease terms to make sure that the property is not vacant. It can take the form of rent-free periods or expenditure to meet the tenant's specific needs. With residential, the developer has the flexibility to sell part of the development to individual purchasers and rent out the balance, therefore not creating pressure to reduce the rent.

Below is a summary comparing the two categories.

| Residential | Commercial |
|---|---|
| Market research localised | Market research based on a macro or regional level |
| Valuation based on supply and demand | Valuation based on the net income of the property |
| Improving value, a lot easier | Limitations to adding value |
| Less sensitive to competition for rental growth | Sensitive to competition from similar building type |
| More opportunities for building improvements | Less opportunities for building improvements |
| Larger purchaser base | Smaller purchaser base |
| Ease of finance | Complex financing |
| More flexibility in exiting | Limited exit strategies |
| Less sophisticated purchaser – shorter negotiations | Sophisticated purchasers – longer negotiations |
| Greater capital growth in boom times | Less capital growth in boom times |
| Shorter vacancy periods | Longer vacancy periods |

From the above analysis, it may seem that there are more risks involved in commercial properties. It is valid if one must generalise. Still, if one is knowledgeable and experienced in the commercial sector, there are better profits to be made.

## CONCLUSION

Deciding which path to follow as an investor or developer and which development sector to undertake (residential or commercial), will depend not only on your financial circumstances but your goals, personality and your self-motivation. If you decide to become a developer rather than an investor, may I advise that success does not come automatically. To kick start a career as a developer, you need to be educated. Knowledge is the key to any successful business. Without education, a developer can and will make many mistakes along the way. After educating yourself through real estate courses or intensive reading, you will have a better understanding of which path you should follow. As for which sector to develop, I would suggest that you start small by undertaking a small residential project and then later to larger projects. After building up your financial resources, knowledge and experience and confidence, you may want to consider commercial developments.

# Chapter 5

# *TIMING, TIMING, TIMING*

## Introduction

In the real estate industry, experts advise that when investing in a property, the vital factor to remember is 'location, location, location'. While this is just as important in the field of real estate development, a more critical factor is 'timing, timing, timing'. Most developments that fail have done so because they have not been timed to correspond with the economic cycle. Developers who introduce their product at a time of oversupply tend to fail as demand has waned, causing a fall in prices, and the developers suffer severe financial losses.

Supply and demand, together with price fluctuations, affect all investment markets. Developers tend to believe that when markets are buoyant, and prices are rising, these conditions will go on forever. Unfortunately, this is not the case, and by failing to develop an understanding of the real estate market cycle, many developers come unstuck.

Putting a timeframe on this cycle is not easy. A conventional theory in the past was that the cycle was seven years in length, but this concept is unfounded. World economies are evolving at a rapid rate and consequently, so are timeframes. The cycle exists not because several years have passed, but because of a combination of factors and influences, such as the state of the economy and social or political issues. The astute developers who can read these signs and market their project at the peak of the cycle have the best chances of making money.

Compared to the erratic performance of the stock market, real estate investment boasts much more predictable market trends. Having a set of future economic expectations makes the forecasting of real estate supply and demand conditions a lot easier. However, real estate cycles differ between property types and urban areas. When examined over time, different property types clearly display dissimilar cyclic behaviours.

As an example, housing markets tend to correspond more closely to the overall economy, while the commercial market does not. Again, in the retail sector, suburban centres reflect current economic trends. Still, regional centres are planned with a longer-term outlook. Urban areas also tend to display differences in their respective positions along the real estate cycle. These result from an area's unique exposure to economic changes and the pace of new development.

In addition to different property types, real estate market cycles may vary from State to State or from city to city. Each area has its micro-economic trends. For example, a new motor plant being established in a specific area will have a significant impact on the economy and the real estate market in that area.

## Factors that affect the timing

Real estate investors look at the timing for a purchase or sale from a different perspective to that of real estate developers. The latter will have to know when to buy a property, and then build, sell or rent their product. For the real estate investor, the process of buying or selling takes less time to settle. In contrast, the real estate developer needs time to plan and then wait for several approvals before his or her project can be marketed. It is, therefore, vitally important in the development industry that you have full knowledge of the real estate market and future trends. While areas of economic, social, environmental and political factors are covered in this book, there may be some extraordinary issues. It can include war, terrorist attacks or protracted union strikes, that can affect the correct timing.

### Economic influence

The general state of the economy has an impact on the demand for housing and other social needs. An economy that has been performing poorly for several years will affect the prosperity and spending power of its people in general. It will have a bearing on their general standard of living and their ability to afford several essential items, including accommodation.

The building industry is thought to be a barometer of the economy. This concept is reinforced by the fact that slow economic growth occurs when building activity declines and strong growth occurs when activity increases. During these growth periods, interest rates are generally low, which causes a demand. Unfortunately, this is usually followed by an increase in rates to suppress the demand and to keep the economy in check. In turn, building material and labour costs increase during periods of growth, and this affects the profit margins and construction periods of new development projects.

When reviewing economic factors, you should look not only at macro-economic trends but also at the micro-level as well. The latter is the local economy surrounding the property to be developed. Factors that can affect economic trends include the following:

- the local employment rates
- growth rates
- inflation
- interest rates
- efficiency of the local government structure
- future planning.

Low unemployment figures (as illustrated in Table 5.1 below) will cause an increase in demand for housing. Still, the reverse is true when these figures increase.

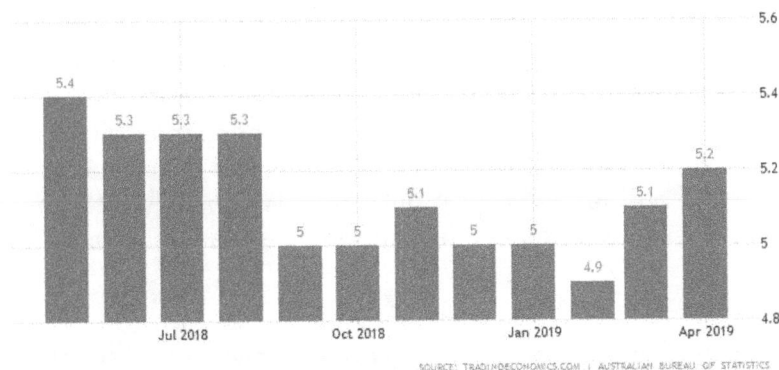

SOURCE: TRADINGECONOMICS.COM | AUSTRALIAN BUREAU OF STATISTICS

Figure 5.1: Unemployment rate: *Australian Bureau of Statistics*

## Social factors

A social factor that you should take into consideration is population growth (as shown in Table 5.2 below). Although Australia's natural population growth is relatively low compared to world standards, it is still fortunate enough to have a steady influx of migrants. These migrants create a demand for housing and other essential services. Also, the population mix can influence urban planning and place pressure in certain areas. Over the past 20 years, we have seen a movement away from smaller rural towns to the city areas as younger people seek better job opportunities. More recently, there have been more inner-city apartments being built, thus increasing the density in these areas.

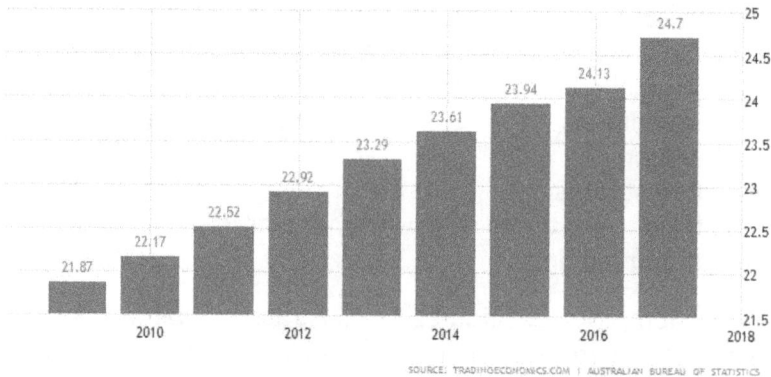

SOURCE: TRADINGECONOMICS.COM | AUSTRALIAN BUREAU OF STATISTICS

Table 5.2 Population growth: *Australian Bureau of Statistics*

The crime rate is another factor that can affect the housing demand of a city or area. If crime (which can be defined as anything from petty offences such as breaking and entering through to government bribery and corruption) is common in a specific area, investors and businesses will avoid it. There is generally movement of the area's law-abiding residents to other less dubious locations.

## Environmental factors

As a result of international concern about sensitive environmental issues, various governments have passed laws to protect the natural resources and ecology of their countries. Any major development attracts interest from environmental and social organisations. The concerns raised can, at times, affect both the feasibility and the timing of the project.

For example, every parcel of land is subject to Australian State's environmental planning policies, regional environmental planning policies, local environmental plans, development control plans, council policies and council resolutions. The Australian Government is also involved by requiring adherence to the Biodiversity and Conservation Act. Under the Integrated Development Approval System (IDAS), concurrent approvals are needed from the relevant government departments such as Agriculture, Fisheries and Forestry (and its Land and Water body), Environment and Heritage, and Transport and Regional Services.

In any 'green fields' project, such as a new subdivision of rural land or a major infrastructure project, there are several studies that should be undertaken. It includes a scoping analysis which identifies public issues and concerns. It assesses the nature and extent of the environmental problems that need to be addressed. Also, undertake an environmental impact study which evaluates the effect on the environment of any introduced factor which could potentially upset ecological balance. Even a conventional rezoning in an urban area can take considerable time to obtain approval as surrounding neighbours may object to the proposal.

## Political factors

Political issues or any changes to government policy or laws can affect decision-making by the public in general. We have often seen that before general elections, the public will delay any major investment decision, such as buying or building a new home. More recently with the 2019 Australian Federal elections, the Labor Government announced changes to negative gearing of rental property rules. It caused concern in the investor market, which slowed the real estate market before the elections. However, when the Liberal Government won the elections, the market started to turn, and confidence was back in the real estate market.

Political stability is another factor that can affect the economic and social spectrum. In recent times we have seen European countries and many parts of Africa experiencing political instability, causing both economic failure and human tragedies.

## The investment cycles

In most investment markets, there is a phenomenon called the 'herd mentality' or 'market sentiment'. It is when the masses blindly follow a few influential investors and end up driving the market's overall direction.

The real estate market is no different. After a building boom where real estate prices have escalated, the market sentiment and therefore, the market moves into a sustained period of negative growth. Usually, several developers and investors get their fingers burnt.

Sooner or later, the excess accommodation that was supplied at the tail end of the boom is taken up. Then there is a sudden need for more housing and commercial buildings. But, by this time there is not enough building activity, as the developers and builders have found other opportunities or changed careers.

As the demand increases, rents start increasing, and people are prepared to pay a lot more for a property. A new band of developers and builders enter the industry to fill the demand. Hearing of the enormous profits being made, more developers and speculators join in. It results in overkill once more and, after the buyers are satisfied, there is again far too much developed property on the market. Prices start falling or flattening, developers lose money, and the cycle starts all over again.

To understand the cycle graphically, you can compare it to a clock (as seen below in Figure 5.1 where 12 o'clock represents the peak of the building boom and 6 o'clock, the bottom of the recession.

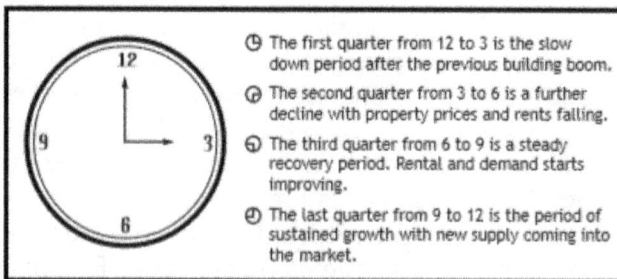

The first quarter from 12 to 3 is the slow down period after the previous building boom.

The second quarter from 3 to 6 is a further decline with property prices and rents falling.

The third quarter from 6 to 9 is a steady recovery period. Rental and demand starts improving.

The last quarter from 9 to 12 is the period of sustained growth with new supply coming into the market.

Figure 5.1: The economic clock

The market cycle can be further described as follows:

- The market in decline (12 to 3 o'clock) — during this phase, the real estate market is becoming oversupplied with new buildings. Prices start to fall, and the buyer is offered concessions.
- The bottom of the market (3 to 6 o'clock) — during this stage, the market is at its worst. No new developments are being built, the concessions offered to buyers and investors are at their highest level and very little economic activity is taking place.
- The growth period (6 to 9 o'clock) — during this period, the economy is starting to pick up, and expansion in all types of business starts to occur. The real estate market is on the rise, and new developments begin to take place.
- The maturity stage (9 to 12 o'clock) — by this stage, the market has matured, and demand is catching up with supply. Prices in real estate will peak and start to stabilise.

### Be one step ahead of the cycle

Astute developers are aware of the above factors. Usually, they act several months or years ahead of the cycle. They are generally active in the last two quarters which is the period of growth and the maturity stage. They buy the properties they intend developing at the bottom of the recession and sell or rent their projects for top prices at the peak of the boom. To follow their footsteps, the novice developer must constantly monitor the movements in the industry and the economy.

## The best time to buy a property to develop

Although it is usually recommended that you buy at the bottom of the market, there is no specific time to buy a property you intend to develop. This depends more upon the negotiations and conditions under which you are offered to purchase the property. For example, if you are aware of possible changes in the town planning of a specific area, you may decide to offer to buy the property conditional upon rezoning. It will give you time to start planning your development. Also, by delaying the settlement, you will not be liable for the holding cost. The best time to purchase a specific property will be contingent on the type of development. For example, a residential building will have different priorities (such as increased zoning densities) compared to those of a commercial building (which may be reliant on a new road layout).

If you have the financial resources, you may buy a property to develop at a later stage and the best time to buy would be when there are bargains around. Factors that cause this situation are high-interest rates or other negative factors, which create an oversupply and a decrease in demand. As buying in the downturn provides the best opportunities to find a bargain whereas during the good times, developers should be planning their strategies for the next slump. They should be selling and cashing up so that they can be selective and negotiate from a strong position.

## Recognise signals for rising markets

One of the early signals of a property price increase is the fall in vacancy rates in rental accommodation in both residential and commercial buildings. These sorts of statistics can be obtained from various associations and research companies involved in the property industry, including the following:
- Property Council of Australia (PCA)
- Real Estate Institute of Australia (REIA)
- Housing Industry Association (HIA)
- Master Builders Associations (MBA).

Several real estate companies, websites and financial institutions provide free online newsletters giving up-to-date information about the real estate market and trends. Some that come to mind include Core Logic (https://www.corelogic.com.au) and Colliers International (https://www.colliers.com.au/find_research).

Higher rental returns and strong demand for new accommodation are music to a real estate developer's ear. If interest rates are low, the developer knows that homebuyers and investors will be attracted to the market. New homebuyers feel a sense of urgency to buy before the prices rise beyond their reach, and investors try to catch the price rise early to make money.

Additional signs of the market improving include the following:

- a sustained growth in prices
- an increase in building plan approvals
- a fall in unemployment
- an expansion of businesses
- an increase in investor and business confidence
- media reports of the rising cost of goods and services.

## Recognise the signals of a falling market

In past economic cycles, one could predict the rise and fall in the real estate market based on early signs of the interest rates movement offered by banking institutions and controlled by the Reserve Bank. However, the recent fall in real estate prices starting in 2017 was not determined by a rise in interest rates. It was mainly due to the oversupply of apartments and a downturn in the mining industry. It is not to say that interest rates do not affect the real estate market as it could happen in the future. When interest rates do increase, the demand for real estate will start to wane, prices will begin to fall, and vacancy rates in rental real estate will increase. Property management agents can detect the early signs of decline, as the rate of enquiry for rental accommodation starts to slow down. Other signs are an increase in unemployment and businesses defaulting and taking longer to pay their bills.

Developers who recognise these signs should take precautions and cease planning for new schemes or starting new buildings. It is to avoid the risk of being stuck with unsold properties or vacant accommodation. Also, during this period, building materials are in short supply, and subcontractors demand higher rates for their services. It is not wise to plan any new developments at this time as you may have sold properties at a fixed price that will eventually cost you more to build.

## The best and worst time to develop

We all wish that we had a crystal ball to predict the best time to develop our properties. Of course, if this were the case, we would all be real estate millionaires! The best we can do is rely on sound information and advice from professionals. Listed below in Table

5.3 are some factors that will assist you in working out the best and worst times to develop.

| BEST TIME TO DEVELOP | WORST TIME TO DEVELOP |
|---|---|
| <ul><li>When interest rates are low</li><li>When building plan approvals are increasing</li><li>When rental demands increase</li><li>When the cost of building material and labour is low</li><li>When businesses start expanding</li><li>When investor confidence is improving</li><li>When employment figures start improving</li><li>When there is an increase in population and migration</li><li>When there are new favourable surrounding public amenities such as new schools and shopping centres</li></ul> | <ul><li>When interest rates are high</li><li>When there is an oversupply of rental</li><li>When there is a shortage of labour and building materials</li><li>When businesses are defaulting or renegotiating their loans</li><li>Bankruptcies are increasing</li><li>Investor confidence is low</li><li>When unemployment figures are rising</li><li>When population and migration figures start dropping</li><li>When there are unfavourable elements such as the decline of a neighbourhood and the increase in crime</li></ul> |

Table 5.3: Best and worst times to develop

## Planning your survival

If you have not timed the cycle correctly, the key to survival during a real estate downturn is to be in a position where you do not have to sell. Even though this was part of your development plan. Developers are exposed to risk when:

- the developer borrows more than 60 per cent of the total development cost
- unsophisticated small to medium developers purchase real estate and start developing at the peak of the boom
- investor developers hold vacant buildings or have inexperienced business tenants.

To survive in real estate development, you must have the financial capability to cover debt and other outgoings until the market swings back to better times. Carefully consider the following vital factors for your survival.

### Leveraging

As I suggested earlier, be smart about borrowing money. High gearing equals high risk. While the concept of financial leveraging is advisable, it only works where the gearing ratio can be sustained during difficult times.

### Quality tenants

If you plan to hold your development as an investment, look for good quality tenants. They should have sound financial backing and can survive an economic downturn.

### Contingency

It makes good business sense to have a cash contingency reserve to withstand the downturn. It could be in the form of access to additional credit or, preferably, personal cash reserves.

## Conclusion

When times are good, try to avoid being swayed or influenced by the general crowd rushing to buy properties. Likewise, try not to think that you are 'missing the boat'. Sit back and take some time to analyse the factors which are driving the market and how the market will react in the next few months or years. I have seen many clients lose profits due to the belief that the market will never slow down. When the market moves into a lull, look for opportunities, but also keep an eye out for improvement in market conditions. Remember that timing is one of the most critical factors for success in real estate development.

# Chapter 6

# THE DEVELOPMENT PROCESS

## Introduction

This chapter gives a broad view of a typical development procedure but does not go into expansive detail on each aspect — if every detail were to be looked at in depth it would fill another book! I have documented the real estate development process in the form of a checklist to highlight the more important aspects. For this exercise, I have used a medium sized housing development (such as a retirement village, an apartment block, or a medium-sized neighbourhood shopping centre) as an example.

## The stages of real estate development

The development process, also shown in Figure 6.1 below can be broken into the following stages:

Stage 1 — Vision
Stage 2 — Concept
Stage 3 — Technical
Stage 4 — Construction
Stage 5 — Implementation.

The time allocated to each stage will vary according to the size and complexity of the project. However, the basic principles of the various stages remain the same.

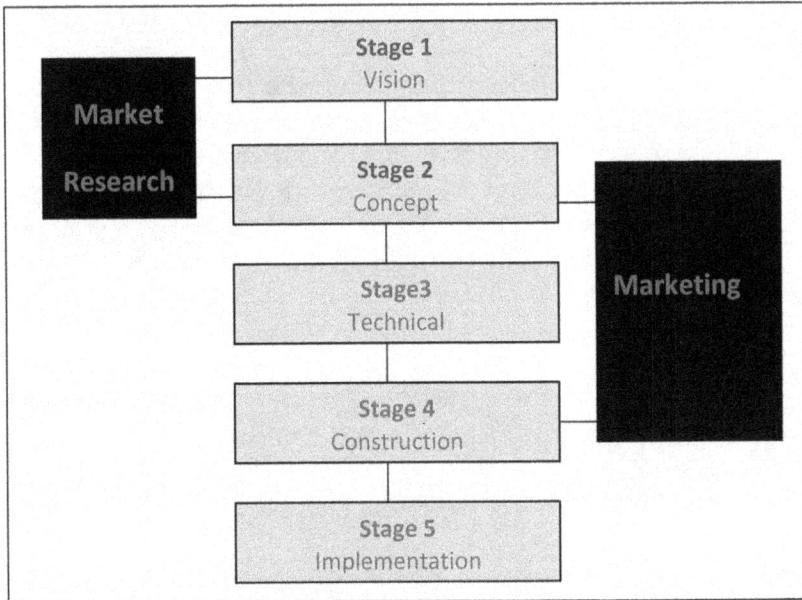

Table 6.1 Diagram of Development Process

## Stage 1 - Vision

Stage 1 is the start of a project where a developer has a vision of a development or is offered an opportunity to develop a property that has arisen from the following possibilities:
- A real estate agent has offered a development property for sale.
- A property is not for sale, but the owner is approached by an agent to sell.
- A property is offered by way of tender or proposal call.

### Considerations

Before deciding to purchase a property or taking an option to purchase, consider and research the following:
- Is there a market for the development?
- How will this development fit into your overall development strategy or business goals?
- Will the project be profitable under current market conditions?
- Will finance for this development be available?

- Is the property already zoned for the intended development?
- Are there any encumbrances on the title such as caveats (restrictions) or easements (rights of way — for example, access to the main sewer line for authorities)?
- What is the correct ownership vehicle for the development?
- Who will be part of the development team?
- On what conditions and at what price should you purchase the property?

In some cases, you may not have the time to research the property in detail, as there may be other purchasers interested in the same property. In this situation, you might consider offering to buy the property with conditions to allow research into the necessary information described above.

### Finance

Before committing to the development, the developer must obtain appropriate finance on favourable terms (unless he or she has internal resources). The developer should look at three levels of funding, namely:

- A loan to purchase the land (if required) and for soft cost such as consultant's fees
- Short-term construction loan for the construction and other development costs
- Long-term loan if the intention is to hold the development as a long-term investment.

Detailed information of the proposed development, as well as the developer's credentials, is essential to obtaining finance from any lending institution.

## Stage 2 – Concept

As soon as your offer has been accepted, you or your appointed development manager and various consultants will have to act immediately and start working on the conceptual plans (architectural sketch plans) and a preliminary feasibility study (that is, a study which determines whether or not the development can be accomplished). Start selecting your development team at this stage (I discuss this team in more detail in the next chapter). Before making the formal appointments, ensure that all consultants have professional indemnity insurance and that the policies are current. The following tasks should be undertaken.

## Market research

Market research or due diligence can be undertaken as a condition to the settlement of the property to be developed. Research is vital in any development and can be done either by the developer, real estate consultants or a specialist market research company. The results of the research will help to work out a development strategy and establish a design and development brief for the various consultants involved in the project.

## Concept sketch plans

After a briefing from the developer, the appointed architect or designer (or, in the case of a land subdivision, a town planner), will start working on various planning and development options. During the planning, the architect will work within the parameters set out in the zoning guidelines and any other restrictions.

If the architect or planner requires any engineering or costing input at this stage, he or she will advise the developer and request the appointment of appropriate consultants.

If the scheme is of a substantial size, you should appoint your professional team early and have a meeting to brief them on the project before the sketch plans are prepared. This meeting is an important one as the input of the various consultants could have a considerable bearing on the design of the overall development. In addition, a program for this stage should be drawn up so that the team can organise their work schedule.

## Preliminary cost estimates

After the completion of the conceptual sketch plans, the quantity surveyor or building estimator will prepare preliminary cost estimates and, if necessary, the preliminary feasibility study. These studies are broad in concept and are, at times, an opportunity for the planners and the rest of the design team to revise certain aspects of their proposals to bring the development within budget and with the accepted returns.

Again, depending on the size of the project, the process of sketching plans and performing preliminary costings could take several meetings until the developer is confident that the development will work and is prepared to go to the next stage.

## Planning approval

Depending on where the development is taking place, certain town councils may require detailed drawings, including all plans, elevations, and site conditions, to be submitted for planning approval. This process can be relatively quick but also could be a long and drawn out affair if the development is a controversial one.

Controversial developments are often frustrated by myriad legal requirements and obligations that prevent them from getting off the ground. There are several organisations from which you must obtain official permission before commencement of construction. Depending on the scale and type of the project, some or all of the following must be consulted for approval:

- non-government — environmentalist groups, community groups, special trusts, historical societies, and ratepayers
- government — federal, state, and local. For example, if the local government does not grant planning approval, you can launch an appeal against the decision with your State Government.

Figure 6.2 below shows the typical stages of obtaining approval for a standard, medium-sized housing development.

```
┌─────────────────────────────────────┐
│          Consultation with          │
│        Architect / Town Planner     │
│            (1 – 2 weeks)            │
└─────────────────────────────────────┘
                  │
┌─────────────────────────────────────┐
│  Preparation of Development Application │
│        by Architect / Town Planner  │
│            (2 – 3 weeks)            │
└─────────────────────────────────────┘
                  │
┌─────────────────────────────────────┐
│       Submission to Local Council   │
│            for processing           │
│            (4 – 6 weeks)            │
└─────────────────────────────────────┘
                  │
┌─────────────────────────────────────┐
│    Period for objections to be raised │
│       and answered by Developer     │
│            (2 – 3 weeks)            │
└─────────────────────────────────────┘
                  │
┌─────────────────────────────────────┐
│  Planning department's recommendation │
│               to Council            │
│            (1 - 2 weeks)            │
└─────────────────────────────────────┘
                  │
┌─────────────────────────────────────┐
│       Preparation of Building Plans │
│            (2 – 4 weeks)            │
└─────────────────────────────────────┘
                  │
┌─────────────────────────────────────┐
│        Approval of Building Plans   │
│            (2 – 3 weeks)            │
└─────────────────────────────────────┘
```

Figure 6.2: Typical Stages of Gaining Development Approval

## Marketing

The marketing of the development can start as soon as the conceptual stage is completed or when construction starts. This will obviously depend on your marketing strategy. In some instances, it is the financier's condition that a percentage of a development is either sold or leased before the formal approval of the development finance.

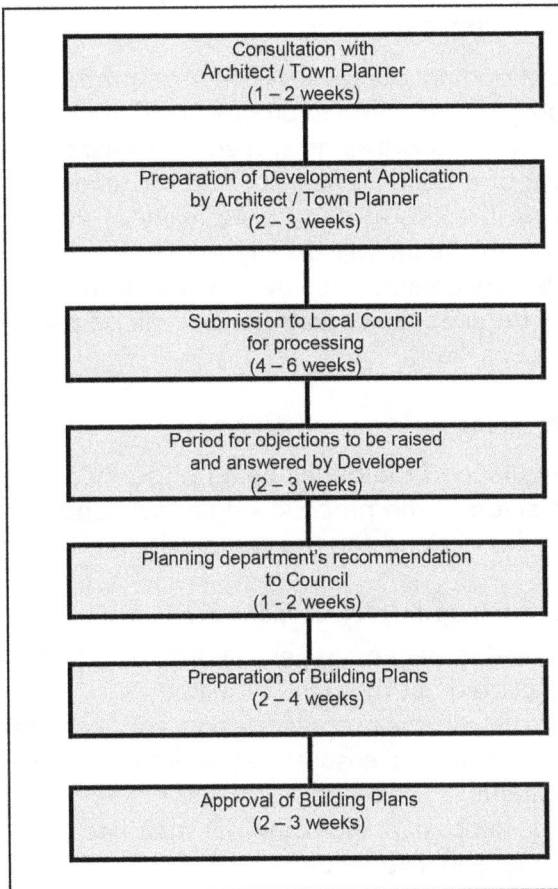

## Stage 3 – Technical

After the development approval has been granted, the various consultants should be instructed to proceed with documentation. This includes the working drawings and specifications for submission and approval of a building licence, and for tendering purposes. Depending on the size and the complexity of the project, each consultant on the team will usually add his or her own aspect to the tender documents. However, if, for example, a specialist contractor is required, a separate tender will be prepared by the appropriate consultant.

### Consultants' roles

Below is an outline of the duties being performed by the consultants at this stage of the process. Additional consultants may be required but this depends on the complexity of the project.

*Development manager (project manager)*
- The development manager will draw up a program of work to be carried out by each consultant.
- He or she will chair regular design and technical meetings with the team to ensure that information flows between consultants.
- The development manager will also keep records of all meetings and instructions.

*Architect (building designer)*
- The architect will prepare working drawings including a site plan, plans, elevations (exterior of the building) and sections (showing construction details).
- If there is no quantity surveyor on the team, the architect will also prepare tender documents, which includes specifications.

*Quantity surveyor*
- If required, the quantity surveyor will prepare a bill of quantities from architects and engineers' drawings.
- He or she will also prepare tender documents.

*Structural engineer*
- The structural engineer will prepare structural drawings in conjunction with the architect's drawings.
- He or she will liaise with and supply information to the architect and quantity surveyor.

*Civil engineer*
- The civil engineer will prepare civil engineering drawings indicating facilities for stormwater drainage, water supply, sewerage, and road and parking details.
- He or she will liaise with and supply information to the architect and quantity surveyor.

*Electrical engineer*
- The electrical engineer will prepare electrical drawings and all electrical layouts.
- He or she will liaise with and supply information to the architect and quantity surveyor.
- The electrical engineer will prepare documents for tender.

*Mechanical engineer*
- The mechanical engineer will prepare mechanical drawings and layouts.
- He or she will liaise with and supply information to the architect and the quantity surveyor.
- The mechanical engineer will also prepare tender documents.

## Tendering

The next stage is the tendering process. This is where the developer selects qualified and experienced builders to submit their quotations for the construction of the building. Each builder is given a set of plans, together with specifications, to quote on. However, on larger scale projects a document known as a bill of quantities is prepared and issued by the quantity surveyor. Most tenders are given a two- to three-week period to be priced and close on at a specific time and day. Any late tenders should not be accepted.

Ensure that your tender includes a clause to state that you, the developer, reserve the right to (if necessary) reject all tenders submitted, even with the most competitive pricing, and make sure you look carefully at each builder's capacity, financial position and the availability of his or her support staff. There are four forms of tendering, and these are discussed below.

*Open or public tender*

The open or public tender is when the tender is open to any builder interested in pricing and building the project. An advertisement is placed in a newspaper or other suitable journal inviting contractors to submit tenders. This format is rarely used as you may have too many builders tendering, making the better builders reluctant to partake in what they may perceive as a lottery. Also, you may not know the full history of the builder you appoint, and this could lead to problems during construction.

*Selected tender*

A more popular format is one where you will select builders recommended to you for their capacity, quality, and experience. Your architect or engineer (who will have had previous experience working with the list of builders) normally makes this recommendation. In this case it is a good idea to select a minimum of three to a maximum of eight tenderers. For highly specialised work, or work in remote areas, there may be only three or four tenderers. The advantage of the selected tender process is that all participants are bidding in the same manner and you can compare prices on an equal basis.

*Registration of interest*

Registration of interest is basically a combination of the above formats. A public advertisement is placed asking contractors to register their interest in pricing and to submit their profiles and experience. This gives the developer the opportunity to check and confirm the capacity and credentials of the interested parties. A few tenderers are then selected to go on to the next stage of submitting a full tender.

*Negotiated contract*

Another format used to obtain a price on the building is a negotiated contract. This is used when a contractor is chosen first and the developer negotiates the best price for the works to be completed. It is always advisable to have someone check the price. On larger contracts, a quantity surveyor would be able to compare the builder's price with other contracts that he or she is involved in.

## The contract

Many institutions, such as the Royal Australian Institute of Architects (RAIA), the Master Builders Association (MBA), the Property Council of Australia (PCA) and the Housing Industries Association (HIA), have standard off-the-shelf contracts readily available. These include the following.

*The lump sum, fixed-price contract*

Under the lump sum, fixed-price contract, the builder must complete the works for an agreed amount and within a specified timeframe. There will be no rise or fall in the contract figure except for any provisional items listed in the contract or for variations during the contract, so keep your variations to a minimum. Extensions of time can be granted on the condition that there are unforeseen circumstances or delays — for example, delays due to inclement weather.

*Lump-sum, rise-and-fall contract*

In a rise-and-fall contract, the builder is protected against the effects of inflation after the tender closes. The selected tenderer is entitled to claim extra payment for any escalation in cost for labour and materials after the tender date. The escalation is calculated through a formula based on the consumer price index or some other agreed point of reference. This type of contract is used in larger projects, and this escalation must be allowed for in your budget. As its name implies, there is also provision for the price to fall under this contract; however, prices generally rise in the building industry.

### Cost-plus contract

Under the cost-plus contract, the builder does not quote a price at the start of the project. The developer agrees to pay the builder the actual cost of the work, plus a fee, for organising and overseeing the project work, including overheads and profit margin. The fee can be a fixed amount or a percentage of the actual cost. There is not much benefit to the developer in using this contract, as he or she will not know the final cost. It only benefits the builder as there is no risk and, as his or her fee is protected, there is no incentive to keep the cost down.

### Schedule of rates contract

The schedule of rates is another form of the cost-plus contract, with the distinction that rates for various items of work are agreed at the outset. It is usually a two-stage selection process. Firstly, the tenderers submit prices for overheads and preliminaries. A tenderer is then chosen to negotiate rates for the construction work. Alternatively, the tenderers can submit rates and mark-up percentages and arrive at a cost estimate based on a provisional bill of quantities. The latter system is also known as a provisional-lump-sum contract. In both systems, the work is then remeasured at the end of the project to arrive at the final price.

### Design and construct contract

Under the design and construct contract, the project is designed and built as a total package for a fixed figure. Most project home builders offer this service for their standard range of plans.

## Notable features of contracts

All contracts are legally exhaustive in nature and if you are unfamiliar with contracts have a lawyer (or architect) examine the document before signing. While all clauses are essential to a contract, listed below are a few to take extra note of:
- Warranties — this will cover which items will have a guarantee and for what period.
- Time schedule — this will include when the on-site work begins and the completion date. There should be a clause to account for inclement weather delays.
- Payment schedule — this will cover when certain payments

are made and at what stage of completion.

- Retention — this section will outline the amount of money to be held back until the building is 100 per cent complete.
- Liens — this will detail what obligations the builder must remove any liens and what lien releases are required. A lien is one person's right to retain that which is in his or her possession but belongs to another until the person in possession's demands is satisfied.
- Prime cost (PC) items and provisional sums (PS) — these should be listed, and the builder's margin noted for handling and profit. These are the estimated cost of items to be selected or works that cannot be accurately priced at the time of the tender and are adjusted as the works progress.
- Variations — this should cover how the cost will be arrived at, including the actual cost and builder's margin for handling, and profit margin.
- Insurance — this should set out what insurance the builder is taking and when the responsibility is to be passed on to you, the developer.

## Stage 4 – Construction

As soon as the development finance is obtained and the contracts signed, construction can commence, and you will need to make sure that all necessary insurance and a building license is in place.

To reduce the potential for problems that may occur during construction, it is good practice to hold a pre-construction meeting with all parties concerned. Outline who is responsible for which parts of the contract and what is expected of each person. Areas that should be covered include:

- the pointing out of site pegs and any other on-site conditions
- access points where the contractor will be able to bring material and equipment on to the site
- a location or facility for the contractor to store materials and equipment on the site
- the proposed construction schedules
- the schedule of site meetings

- daily clean-up requirements
- security requirements
- the procedure for instigating variations to the contract
- the procedure for issuing invoices and progress payments.

## Supervision

Some developers, to save money, do not want consultants to supervise the construction process. It could be a bad error as most consultants have documented the drawings and can, therefore, identify any potential problems or mistakes that may occur on-site. By appointing consultants to supervise their portion of work, you are making them responsible for it and, in doing so, lessening the burden upon yourself if a dispute with the builder arises.

## Site meetings

Site meetings, which are mainly technical in nature, are generally held on a fortnightly or weekly basis, depending on the contract. These meetings involve the supervising development team, the contractor and any other persons involved in the technical issues. The development (or project manager) or the architect acts as the chairperson of these meetings. Minutes are recorded, and all discussions must end with a schedule of actions to be undertaken by specific people to prevent any potential misunderstanding and to ensure that the construction progresses according to the set program.

It is essential that all parties present at the meeting share a common understanding of the goals of the project, including the scope, budgets and, importantly, the timeframes and deadlines.

# Stage 5 – Implementation

When the construction is completed, the appointed architect or project manager will prepare a snag list for any incomplete or irregular finishing items. Ensure that you receive copies of all warranties and guarantees from the contractor. Depending on whether the developer intends holding or selling his development, some or all the following will take place.

## Marketing

The marketing of a development project can be started at any stage of the above development process. Most developers, to lessen their risk may decide to sell the project off-plan when all the architectural plans and development cost have been completed. On the other hand, if they find that the market is sophisticated and would somewhat physically see what they are buying, the developer will only start marketing when the development is completed.

## Sales contracts

The sales contracts can be produced in a variety of formats and are dependent upon the development and at what stage the development or units are sold. If the development is sold "off-plan", the sale will be subject to the completion of the buildings. Whereas if the buildings are completed, a sales contract can be prepared by your attorney or your real estate agent. They may use a standard contract that is available through the local real estate institute.

## Leasing contracts

If the decision is to hold the development as a long-term investment, the developer can have their lawyer prepare a lease agreement. Alternatively, there are standard leasing contracts that are available from the local real estate institute. If a property management company is employed, they would have contracts that have been standardised.

## Settlement of sales

An appointed settlement agent, conveyancer or attorney will settle and transfer the properties sold to contracted purchasers. They will ensure that the purchaser's finance is in place, adjust cost such as rates and taxes to the relevant parties. They would then pay the lending institution who provided the development finance, deduct fees due to them and pay the balance to the developer. The appointed company must be efficient to handle the settlement as any delays will cost interest on money borrowed.

## Property management

The developer, his staff or a specialist management company can undertake the management of the property. It will be dependent or your personal time or the size of the property. The manager will screen potential tenants and negotiate the lease. Also, he or she will prepare an operating budget and establish both management and maintenance policies. During the tenancy, regular visits should be made to the property to ensure that the tenants are taking care of your investment.

## Accounting

After the completion of the development, with buyers or tenants taking occupancy and all sales settled, your accountant will assess your tax position including the adjustment of any outstanding Goods & Services Tax (GST). As most developers are dealing with large sums of money, they will invariably be registered for GST. During construction, the developer will claim the GST component from material purchased and services provided. After the sale and settlement of the development, the developer must ensure that he has the cash to pay the GST to the taxation office. Note that the developer cannot claim the GST component if the intention is to hold a project as a long-term investment.

# Conclusion

Depending on the scale of a project, a substantial amount of time and money is required to ensure that each stage of the development process is completed successfully. A developer can employ several people to take care of this process, but this is money out of the developer's pocket. This type of approach is suitable for larger commercial projects, but not viable for smaller residential schemes where there is a lower profit margin. Besides, the developer should be involved in every stage of the process. He or she will then have a finger on the pulse and have superior control over the project to ensure its eventual success.

Remember, to be a successful developer, you need to follow all aspects of the development process. Your objective during each phase is to minimise assumptions and base your decision-making on the most accurate information. The quality of work accomplished during the process will minimise your risk and set in motion the forces needed for a quality development.

# Chapter 7

# SELECTING A DEVELOPMENT TEAM

## Introduction

There are no short cuts in real estate development, and you should always seek the advice of a professional to discuss your proposals. When it comes to real estate development, treat it like buying your first home and consult the experts. A development should only go ahead after you have carefully assessed your current financial position. It should be followed by examining how the development would fit into your overall business strategy and received expert advice from industry professionals. To save money, some developers do not seek such professional guidance and subsequently make bad decisions. The result is that it cost them more than what they would have saved in the end.

## Selecting the right consultants

Real estate development covers a broad and diverse range of buildings with associated features, which has created a need for specialist consultants who operate in specific areas. Before appointing a consultant, ask for a profile of the person or company to ensure that they have the knowledge, expertise and experience to work on the type of project you intend building. For example, it is pointless hiring a small architectural practice with only residential experience to design a multimillion-dollar shopping centre. Besides not having the background expertise, the smaller practice would not have the staff to service the development. Only appoint consultants who:
- are best qualified for the job
- work or have worked on similar projects to the one you are proposing

- have the qualified staff to support the size of your project
- have worked with you previously and you, therefore, know their capabilities
- have been referred to you by another professional
- have been in business for a satisfactory period
- have been through a selection process.

## Number of consultants

It may not be necessary to hire all the consultants listed in this chapter, as the type of project will determine the type and number of consultants that should be involved. Most consultants offer the complete range of services from inception to completion; however, depending on the size of the project to be tackled, the consultant's scope and brief may be limited to the stage of the project where his or her expertise is required. For example, if you are speculating on renovating older homes, only the services of an architect or building designer, together with a structural engineer with a limited brief, may be required. A quantity surveyor or building estimator would not be necessary as your architect or designer would be able to provide some cost estimates.

## Fees

Most professional consultants have a standard structure for fees as set out by their association or institute but, depending on the level of service, these fees are negotiable. Fees are generally charged as an agreed lump sum or as a percentage of the development construction cost. Understandably, most developers aim to reduce costs to improve profit margins. Still, you should be fair when negotiating a fee for your projects. While it is not always the case, if the negotiated fee is too low, you will not bring out the best in the consultant. They may give more attention to the better-paid projects. Always ensure when dealing with consultants that you have every discussion and agreement in writing, especially the confirmation of fees and the conditions of appointment.

## Disbursements

In addition to fees charged, most consultants would charge for general disbursements, including the cost of travel beyond a certain radius, prints, photocopies, postage, emails and any other expenses beyond the agreed fee. Ensure that you obtain rates for these costs and ask for a record or breakdown if you feel that you have been unfairly charged.

### Professional indemnity insurance

Mistakes can happen on any building project, and even the best professional consultants can be responsible for negligence. It is therefore important that the consultants you employ have current professional indemnity insurance in place.

Professional indemnity cover provides protection against the risk of substantial financial losses. Still, if a consultant does not have a policy in place and is found negligent, you may have to sue the consultant in his or her personal capacity to recover these losses. It may be found that the consultant does not have the assets to back up the damage incurred through the negligence.

### Build a team of professional advisers

After you have selected the consultants you are comfortable with, it is essential to ensure that the group works as a team. As these professionals must work together, any personality conflicts will be detrimental to the project. As a developer, you should be aware of any problems that could arise and resolve them as soon as possible. As well as building the right team, you must feel comfortable that the consultants are serving you to the best of their ability. You should feel pleased that you can call on them at any time when a problem or concern arises.

## Types of professional consultants

As I mentioned earlier, the complexity of the development will determine the number of consultants on the team. At times, consultants will focus on one set task, or a single team member may handle several duties. Listed below are possible consultants who may be involved in a development project.

### Attorney/solicitor

An experienced attorney with sound knowledge in real estate law can guide the developer through all the legal implications of real estate development. He or she can provide the following services:

- drafting of all legal documents, including real estate contracts, lease agreements and partnership agreements
- reviewing of any complex zoning or rezoning matters, finance documents, environmental objections, and service or guarantee agreements
- representing the developer in any legal disputes with purchasers, tenants or contractors.

The fees charged by an attorney are usually based on a flat rate for a specific service, an hourly rate for the work performed or a percentage of a transaction. Qualified attorneys have been accepted by the bar, and they must abide by the rules and code of ethics of the Law Society of Australia.

## Accountant

An accountant can assist the developer with all matters relating to the financial and tax aspects of real estate development. His or her services can include:

- determination and assessment of the best ownership vehicle
- assessment of the tax structures
- preparation of monthly operating statements
- preparation of annual audited financial records and tax returns
- representation of the developer in the case of a tax audit.

Qualified accountants belong to either the Institute of Chartered Accountants or the CPA Australia.

## Development manager

If you do not have enough time available or if you are a novice developer, a development manager can assist or manage a project on your behalf. Development managers usually are employed on larger or complex projects and can be confused with a project manager. A development manager is an expert on all development matters, and his or her services include:

- preparation of overall development and investment strategy

- performance of complete management duties and acting as the principal-agent on behalf of the owner/developer
- appointment and management of consultants where necessary
- preparation and establishment of the brief to all consultants
- supervision of the preparation of a feasibility study
- procurement of finance for the project
- monitoring of the construction of the development
- supervision of the marketing of the development.

There is no peer body or institute for development managers. However, most development managers charge a fee based on a percentage of the value of the development or the construction cost.

## Project Managers

Project managers are employed to manage the professional team and the building contract on behalf of the developer or development manager. They should be appointed before any of the other professional team members so that they are able to advise the developer or development manager on the best professional team for the project. The role of the project manager is to assist the developer or development manager with:

- negotiation and appointment of consultants and execution of consultant contracts
- organise the design team to optimise the design by analysing various options in technical and economic terms
- arrange for supervision and construction of the works and execution of the building contractor contract
- prepare of cash-flows, handle construction claims and payment settlement upon completion, organise completion acceptance and transfer of as-built files to the owner.

Depending on the level of service required, fees are charged as a percentage of the construction or on a time basis. The professional body that most project managers belong to is the Australian Institute of Project Management.

## Architect

The architect's role in a development is essential, as he or she can put your ideas on paper and turn them into a reality. An architect can provide the following services:

- professional design consultation
- recommendation of other professional consultants
- preparation of conceptual sketch plans, presentation drawings and models
- preparation of working drawings, specifications and tender documents
- contract administration and on-site supervision.

The Royal Australian Institute of Architects (RAIA) sets out the fee guidelines charged by architects. The fees are charged on a percentage basis of the total building cost or on a time charge basis for partial services.

## Building designer

Most building designers concentrate on the residential sector of the building industry. Still, there is a small percentage who specialise in the commercial sector. They perform similar duties to architects but do not hold an architectural degree; however, some may have a diploma or certificate in drafting or architectural design. Some designers who specialise in a specific area are highly efficient and knowledgeable and, at times, due to their experience and technical knowledge, are better equipped than architects.

Fees charged are like the scale used by architects but could be a little less. There are several associations that these designers may belong to, including the Building Designers Association of Australia.

## Quantity surveyor/building estimator

A quantity surveyor or building estimator plays an essential role in a development as his or her estimation of the cost will determine whether the project should proceed or not. When selecting a quantity surveyor, make sure that he or she is experienced in the type of project you are developing. A surveyor with limited expertise in a specific development type may underestimate or overestimate costs. Quantity surveyor's services include:

- preliminary cost estimates
- feasibility studies including cash flows
- production of bills of quantities
- cost control, including verification of payment certificates during construction.

Like architects, the quantity surveyor's fees are based on the guidelines set out by their professional institute, the Australian Institute of Quantity Surveyors. Their fees are based on a percentage of the building cost or on a time charge for partial services.

## Town planners

Town planners are generally required on larger development schemes where urban planning or rezoning of the property is required or on complex and controversial projects. They can provide the following services:
- application and documentation of reasons for rezoning
- urban and township planning
- reporting on future development structures.

Fees are based on a percentage of the development cost or a time charge according to the guidelines as set out by their institute. Bodies that govern the professional ethics of planners are the Royal Australian Planning Institute or the Australian Institute of Urban Studies.

## Structural engineer

Structural engineers are used wherever structural information is required. They generally work under the architect or designer's direction. In the case of industrial buildings, they act as principal-agent. Their services include:
- design, drawing and specification of structural concrete elements
- design, drawing and specification of structural steel elements
- budget costing of structural work
- evaluation and reporting on the structural stability of existing buildings
- on-site supervision.

Fees are determined as a percentage of the cost of the structural elements or on a time basis, which is based on guidelines set out by their professional body. Structural and other consulting engineers are members of the Association of Consulting Engineers, Australia.

## Hydraulic and civil engineers

Hydraulic engineers are involved with the design of fluid movement systems. Although they are not often required on simple residential projects, their advice can be necessary if a complex or restricted water supply, sewerage or drainage systems are involved. The work can also be undertaken by a civil engineer who generally works on the external elements of a building such as stormwater, drainage, water supply, roads and parking areas. As with structural engineers, they work under the direction of the architect. Hydraulic and civil engineers can provide:

- a report on the availability of existing services to a property
- the design, drawing and specifications for stormwater, drainage, water and general external works
- a budget cost to all civil work and on-site supervision
- on-site supervision.

Fees are charged as a percentage of the cost of the civil work or on a time basis for partial services.

## Electrical engineer

Electrical engineers take care of all electrical requirements in a development. Their services include:

- design, drawing and specification of all electrical requirements, both internally and externally on a project
- provision of budgets and separate tender documents
- on-site supervision if required.

Fees are again based on a percentage of the cost of the electrical work or on a time basis.

## Mechanical engineer

Mechanical engineers are used when any mechanical work for the development is required to be independently designed and documented for tender. The types of mechanical work on a building that these engineers can oversee include air-conditioning, heating, fire-fighting facilities, lifts and escalators. They can provide:

- design and documentation for all or part of the mechanical requirements
- budgets and a separate tender to the main documents
- on-site supervision if required.

Fees are determined similarly to those of the engineers discussed above.

### Land surveyors

Land surveyors are trained to record accurate dimensions and document topographical information both before and after a development. Their services include:

- aerial surveys and town planning information
- topographical and contour feature surveys
- strata plan drawings and titles.

Fees charged are dependent on the size of the project and the work involved. It is best to obtain a quote before appointing a land surveyor.

### Real estate agent

A real estate agent can assist you with the following:

- listing properties available for development
- specific property and development information
- market information such as present and future prices in real estate
- the sale and marketing of a development
- the leasing of rental development.

Real estate agents charge a commission for their services. A standard range of fees is set out by each State's Real Estate Institute, but fees are usually negotiable.

### Property valuer

A property valuer calculates or estimates the current market value of a property according to precedent. When a developer is applying for finance, the lender will require a sworn valuation from a qualified and accredited valuer. Property valuers can provide valuations on the following:

- the current value of a property for a finance institution
- the current value of a property for the taxation office
- the current replacement value of a property for an insurance company.

The fees charged by valuers can range from a few hundred dollars for a single-family home to a few thousand dollars for larger properties.

## Finance broker

If you need various options for financing or alternative sources of funding for your project, consult a finance broker. He or she will have:

- the specialist knowledge of who the best lenders are for a specific project
- access to the best interest rates and charges
- knowledge of how to present a project and to negotiate the best terms and conditions.

Most brokers charge a success commission for their services. Alternatively, their fee is paid by the bank or lender. The commission is based on a percentage of the loan proceeds and is dependent on the size or the loan and whether it is debt or equity.

## Advertising and marketing agent

For smaller projects, a real estate agency can handle the marketing for housing developments; however, on larger development projects, a marketing company may be required. A marketing company can handle the following:

- reviewing the current market conditions on the type of development envisaged
- reviewing the current market mix (that is, age, gender, income group and race) and preparing a marketing strategy
- setting a marketing budget for the length of the project
- assisting in a public relations program
- preparing graphic design and presentation work.

Fees are generally charged on a time or percentage basis. It is advisable to confirm all fees before the appointment.

## Insurance broker

An experienced insurance broker who understands real estate and development matters can save money in terms of insurance on a building development. The broker should review your current policies on the development and should provide:

- appropriate replacement cost insurance for the completed development
- public liability insurance
- rental loss insurance in the case of an investment development
- contractor's 'all risk' policy if you are subcontracting.

The insurance company providing the policy pays the insurance broker's commissions, and insurance brokers are paid only when a policy is sold.

## Property manager

If the development is to be held as a long-term investment and rented out, it is advisable to employ a property manager or a management company. They have specific management skills and have the required expertise to oversee the property. The services property managers provide are:

- establishment of an operating account
- collection of all rentals
- taking care of all maintenance items and tenant problems
- payment of all invoices and expenses relating to the property
- preparation of all monthly accounting statements required by the property owner
- preparation of quarterly and annual budgets.

Generally, a property manager's service charge is based on a percentage of the collected rental income. Their fees can range from 2.5 per cent to 8 per cent and is dependent upon the type and size of the property to be managed. These fees are negotiable and, at times, both parties can agree upon a flat fee. Property managers should be members of the Property Council of Australia or the Real Estate Institute of Australia.

## Other consultants

At times, other professional consultants may be needed where specialist knowledge is required. These might include:

- *Market Researcher* - for analysis of the characteristics of the market and the demographic profile of targeted market that will occupy the building
- *Conveyancer/settlement agent* — for the transfer and settlement of the property. Some agents are members of the Australian Institute of Conveyancers.
- *An environmental consultant* — for environmental issues such as reports on the impact of a development site on the environment.
- *Geo-technical engineer* — for soil and ground testing. These professionals are members of the Australian Institute of Geoscientists.
- *Traffic engineer* – for assessment of traffic access and egress and analysis of parking requirements.
- *Fire engineer* – for advice on compliance on any fire-related matters within the building
- *Landscape architect* — for landscape design.
- *Interior designer* — for consultation on the design of interiors.
- *Building certifier* - for building compliance advice

# CONCLUSION

The list of people and professionals who make up a development team may seem exhaustive. However, the number of consultants you take on will depend on the extent to which you want to be involved in the real estate development game. Also, the size and type of development will determine and the number of consultants. As a full-time developer, you should be continually looking out for new opportunities, and a strong development team is essential for success. If your initial project is small (for example, a residential duplex unit development), you may only require the services of an architect or building designer and a structural engineer. In contrast, for a regional shopping centre, you will likely utilise the services of most the consultants discussed in this chapter.

# Chapter 8

# THE IMPORTANCE OF A FEASIBILITY STUDY

## Introduction

A feasibility study can be likened to a business plan. It will not only assist in reducing your risks but will be an aid to any finance you may require for a project. More importantly, it will make you and your financier feel more confident in your ability to succeed in the venture. Some developers claim that they rely on their intuition and so do not need an intensive investigation into their proposed development. While this approach may be acceptable in smaller residential projects, this method will result in failure on much larger commercial projects.

## Why prepare a feasibility study?

One of the most important steps before launching any new development project is a well-constructed feasibility study. Such a study must include, among other things, the goals for the project, a description of the project, and the expected return. Preparing a comprehensive study takes a considerable amount of time and effort but once completed, the study will serve as a guide to follow, not only for the developer but also for the development team, which includes consultants and financiers or investors. In preparing the study there will be several other important benefits the developer can anticipate such as:

### Testing the concept

The systematic approach to the study will allow the developer to make his mistakes on paper, rather than when the project is completed. Cost overruns can eventually result in a failed development and can possibly bankrupt the developer leaving several businesses involved in the project with bad debts.

## Confidence

A comprehensive feasibility study will make the developer feel more confident in his ability to proceed with the development. At times, it may even compensate for a lack of capital and experience, if there are several factors in favour of the developer, such as a sound concept and significant market demand for the scheme.

## Finance

Most development projects will require financing and a feasibility study will show what level of finance will be required, and when and for how long it will be required. Under-capitalisation and early cash flow problems in a project are two major reasons why new developments fail. To bankers and potential investors, the study will help to communicate your ideas and it will help them understand and appreciate the reasoning behind these ideas.

## Developer's equation

In broad terms, the common approach to a feasibility analysis or study is the developer's equation that considers factors such as land costs, building costs and finance costs with the likely returns from the completed project. The equation can be described as:

$$\textit{Value = land costs + building costs + finance costs + developer's profit}$$

The value of the development is based upon capitalisation of the net income and land, building and finance costs and more thorough methods of calculations are described in more detail under this chapter.

# Calculating your development profit

When real estate developers assess the financial viability of a potential project, they must account for all cost factors associated with the project. Some of the cost factors can be predetermined, for example the costs of construction, professional fees and marketing. In many instances most of the costs associated with the uncertainties and risks of real estate development can only be guessed at. Clearly the costs associated with such risks may vary greatly, and if the most negative result arises where there is a range of possible outcomes, the consequences may well be extremely traumatic for the real estate developer.

It follows that where there is a risk associated with a development there is a requirement that the returns earned should exceed the returns that could be earned on risk-free investments such as Government Bonds.

### The greater the risk, the bigger the return that is required

There are several terms used such as discounted cash flow, present value factors, and internal rate of return, and more. These are formulas used for larger commercial projects and they can be quite confusing to the novice developer. While I explain these in my commercial real estate development handbook, we must remember that the bottom line in evaluating the returns from real estate development consist of only two particularly important factors: "cash flow" and "net profit".

These formulas do not apply to all projects depend on your development strategy. For example, if you were developing a residential project to sell and where the purchasers are buying for personal use, your main interest would be the residual profit at the end of the project, which is achieved by calculating your sales figures less your total expenditure. On the other hand, if you were building a commercial building to sell to a major investor, you would use a capitalisation rate to calculate the end value of the building.

In the rest of this chapter we will look at the various formulas that can be used to analyse the viability of a project.

## Residual profit

This formula is used for simple developments and as rule of thumb:

| | |
|---|---|
| Gross sales revenue | $_____ |
| *Less* selling expenses | $_____ |
| Net sales proceeds | |
| *Less* development cost | $_____ |
| Net taxable proceeds | $_____ |
| *Less* taxes | $_____ |
| Residual profit | |

This accounting system can be illustrated by the example below. Assumed Gross sales revenue ($1,000,000), Selling expenses ($60,000), Development cost ($500,000), Land     cost ($200,000) and Taxation rate (say 30%)

| | |
|---|---|
| Gross sales revenue | $1,000,000 |
| Less selling expenses | $    60,000 |
| Net sales proceeds | $  940,000 |
| Less development cost | $  500,000 |
| Less land cost | $  200,000 |
| Net taxable proceeds | $  240,000 |
| Less tax | $    72,000 |
| Residual profit | $  168,000 |

Therefore, the profit margin on the development cost is:

$$\frac{\$168,000}{\$700,000} \times 100 = 24\%$$

## Formula to establish the value of a development site

Before purchasing a piece of land for development, a financial viability of development project is assessed using an equation such as this:

**Profit = sales revenue – cost of development – cost of land**

that is

**P = R – C - L**

The developer will make an estimate of the sales revenue and cost of construction, and will set a profit "hurdle rate", the achievement of which will result in the project being considered viable. The cost of land (the price the developer will be willing to pay for the property) will be a variable in the equation. The following two examples illustrate the effect of different profit requirements on the cost of land:

### Example 1 – low risk development

Hurdle rate profit required:      24% of cost of development

Estimated revenue from sales:  $ 10m

Estimated cost of construction: $ 6m

Substituting the equation $P = R - C - L$

> *Gives 0.24 (C + L) = R – C - L*
>
> $L = \dfrac{R - 1.24\,C}{1.24} = \dfrac{10 - (1.24 \times 6)}{1.24}$
>
> *L = $2.06m*

In this low risk development, the real estate developer will be willing to pay $2.06 million for the land.

### Example 2 – high-risk development

Hurdle rate profit required: 35% of development cost
Other factors remain the same. In this case:

> $L = \dfrac{R - 1.35C}{1.35} = \dfrac{10 - (1.35 \times 6)}{1.35}$
>
> *L = $1.41m*

In the high-risk development, the real estate developer will not be willing to pay more than $1.41 million for the land. The physical attributes of the land may be identical in both instances, but the perception that the second development is riskier than the first results in a 32 per cent reduction in the value of the second piece of land.

It follows that to achieve a high selling price for developable land, it is vital that as many as possible of the uncertainties and risks associated with the development of the land are eliminated.

Please note that the percentages used in the above examples are not cast in stone and will vary according to several factors such as competition for the land, the prevailing interest rates and other comparable returns on investment.

## Property measurements

When purchasing land for development or selling your development, reference is made to the appraised per unit of area to determine and compare values. This method is used more as a guide in the early analysis of a development as there are other factors such as parking, building lines, height restrictions, topography, easements, and so on, that could affect the real value per unit area.

### Price per square metre

The price per square metre is derived by dividing the asking price or appraised value by the total square metres of the property.

$$\frac{\textit{Selling price or appraised value}}{\textit{Total square metres}} = \textit{Price per square metre}$$

In comparing various buildings, be sure to use the same basis for measuring as they can be measured in the following different ways:

- *Gross square metres* – This is the total square meters of a building and includes all areas such as leased areas, passages, stairways, toilet facilities, etc. and is measured to the external skin of the building.

- *Net leasable area* – This is area that is leased to tenants and does not include common areas such as passages, stairways, etc.

## Price per unit

The price per unit is calculated by dividing the selling price or appraised value by the number of units on a property. This calculation is normally applied to residential developments.

$$\frac{\textit{Selling price or appraised value}}{\textit{Number of units}} = \textit{Price per unit}$$

If you are developing higher density residential units or apartments it is important to compare the price per unit of land value, you are paying. Check the zoning as you may be paying the same price per square metre for the same land area but because the second property may have a different zoning you may be allowed to develop with a few units less. This will affect the profitability of the development.

## Price per plot ratio metre

The price per plot ratio metre benchmark is derived by dividing the selling price or appraised value by the allowable plot ratio area for a development site. This benchmark is mainly used in the development of commercial buildings.

$$\frac{\textit{Selling price or appraised value}}{\textit{Plot ratio area}} = \textit{Price per plot ratio metre}$$

Most commercial development sites have zoning criteria with a certain allowable plot ratio. In purchasing this type of site always check the price per plot ratio metre, as it will differ from the price per square metre and from property to property.

## Market valuation methods

Every developer would like to know the possible estimated market value or sales figure that is achievable at the completion of the development project. There are three approaches in determining the development's value:

1. Direct market comparison.
2. The actual cost approaches.
3. The income approach.

## 1. Direct market comparison

This method is useful in the valuation of undeveloped sites and housing developments. The process would be used to analyse similar and recently sold properties and compare them with the proposed new development. The projected sale figure should be adjusted to account for any differences with the new proposal.

*Sales of comparable properties +/-- adjustments = estimated market value of development*

Once the estimated value has been calculated, the developer would deduct the construction and land cost to give an estimated profit.

*Estimated market value – construction and land cost = estimated profit*

## 2. The actual cost approach

This approach would be to estimate the construction cost together with the land cost and then add a profit margin relative to the risk level of the project.

*Estimated construction cost + land cost + % profit margin = estimated market value*

This method is not regarded favourably by most real estate developers as it does not value the true acceptable market value and the developer could be stuck with buildings he cannot sell.

## 3. The income approach

The income approach is a valuation method that enables a development to be valued on a basis of quality and quantity. Two steps have to be taken: firstly, the net operating income potential of the rental space must be estimated with comparative properties; secondly, the capitalisation rate must be determined by comparing the rate of return obtainable on alternative investments with similar characteristics. The net estimated income is then divided by the determined capitalisation rate to calculate the proposed market value.

### Step 1- net operating income (NOI)

In order to calculate the NOI, one has to firstly analyse the gross potential income (GPI), which is the total potential income that can be generated by the development and secondly to deduct a possible vacancy rate and the net operating expenses (OE).

| | |
|---|---|
| *Gross potential income (GPI)* | $_____ |
| *Less vacancy rate % (VR)* | $_____ |
| *Less operating expenses (OE)* | $_____ |
| *Net operating income (NOI)* | $_____ |

Where
- *Gross potential income (GPI)* is the sum of all income derived from a development and this includes:
  o All rental income based on per unit (residential) or per square metre (commercial); and
  o Miscellaneous income such as parking, cleaning, garden maintenance, etc.
- *Vacancy rate (VR)* is based on a percentage factor that will fluctuate with the type of development and the current market conditions.
- *Operating expenses (OE)* is the sum of expenses incurred to operate the completed property daily, which include:
  o Fixed expenses. These expenses are fixed in cost and therefore more predictable and include items such as council rates, insurance, property management, etc.; and
  o Variable expenses. These items vary with time and include expenses such as repairs and maintenance, marketing, supplies, leasing commissions, etc.

*Step 2 – capitalisation rate (CR)*

The capitalisation rate or yield is the rate of return on the value of the property. Each type of property will have a different capitalisation rate, based on the associated risk and the level of management required. Remember the greater the risk in the development the higher the capitalisation rate. Before you embark on using a capitalisation rate fully investigate the going rate for the type of property you are developing and in the location of your proposal. Listed below is a range of sample capitalisation rates used in the real estate industry at the time of writing. This is only a sample and should be investigated before use.

- o Residential     3.0% to 6.0%
- o Offices     5.5% to 7.0%
- o Retail     5.0% to 7.5%
- o Industrial     5.5% to 9.0%

*Step 3 – the calculation*

Using the above information, you can now use the following formula to calculate the value of the proposed development.

**Value (V) = net operating income (NOI) / capitalisation rate (CR)**

Example:     Assume a small office block development
Net operating income = $145,000.pa
Capitalisation rate = 7%

**Value     = $145,000 / 0.07 = $2,071,429**

Some well-established developers specialising in commercial buildings aim to sell to institutional investors. These developers will look for the maximum achievable net operating income with the least capital cost incurred, therefore showing a high capitalisation rate or return on capital. They will sell the development to an institutional investor at a lower capitalisation rate before starting construction therefore reducing their risk and beneficial development cent financing. Using the above example, if the developer shows an 8.5 per cent net return and sells the building to an investor who wants a 6 per cent return, the developer will make a pre-tax profit of $365,547 as seen by the example below:

- o   Value = $145,000 / 0.085 = $1,705,882 (which is the developer's capital cost)
- o   Therefore: $2,071,429 less $1,705,882 = $365,547 profit
- o   This represents a 21.43% profit on capital cost $365,547 / $1,705,882)

## Trends significant to sale prices.

In estimating the projected sale prices in a development, attention should also be paid to changes in trends and factors that may affect the supply and demand for real estate, and not only to estimating the yearly gross incomes. The following list gives examples of factors that could alter existing trends and therefore affect supply and demand.

### Changes in economic variables

- Changes in employment rates.
- Changes in the business cycle.
- Changes in new technology affecting employment.

### Changes in local economic structure

- Neighbourhood decline.
- Shifts in local primary industries.

### Changes in household formation

- Changes in childbearing expectations.
- Changes in population age group distribution.
- Changes marriage arrangements.

### Changes in consumer trends

- Preference for a certain style.
- Preference for certain amenities.
- Preference for location.

### Changes in government policies

- Taxation laws.
- Environmental issues.
- Development limitations.

### Changes in financing techniques

- New capital raising devices.
- Syndicates.
- Property trusts.

### Changes in town planning structure

- Urban renewal.
- New zoning changes.
- Transport systems.

### Changes in technology

- Telecommunications.
- Computers and Internet.

## Constructing your feasibility presentation

A winning feasibility study is one that assists in accomplishing the developer's objectives, whether it is to obtain a better understanding of the project, its viability or to raise additional finance. The layout and content of the study can be split up into manageable sections to be carried out by the developer and his team of professional consultants and advisors.

A common approach in a feasibility study is to cover important factors such as land cost, building costs and finance cost and the return on the development. In supporting these factors, the following components should be incorporated in the study:

1. The description of the property to be developed.
2. The description of the proposed development.
3. A market research report.
4. The total development cost.
5. Programme from inception to completion.

6. The complete financial analysis including its sensitivity levels.
7. A real estate valuation.
8. A marketing strategy.
9. A final recommendation.

If the developer is applying for finance, then he or she would add the following to the above:

10. A set of financial figures including balance sheets.
11. 1 A history of the developer's previous experience.

## 1. Description of the property to be developed

The following information should be included under this section:
- The location of the property (a locality map will help).
- Property dimensions and site area (a survey plan will help).
- Lot number and title references.
- Legal tenure of land (Torrens Title, Crown Tenure, Native Title, etc.).
- Encumbrances such as easements and mortgages.
- Existing improvements if any.
- Description of adjacent properties.
- Soil conditions (a report from a geo-technical engineer).
- Availability of essential services (water, sewerage, gas, electricity, etc.).
- Town planning zoning and regulations.

## 2. Description of the proposed development

This section can be prepared by the developer or by his architect and should include the following:
- Description of the overall project.
- Description of important details of the proposal.
- The site plan.
- Plans (can be reduced to a scale but must be readable).
- Elevations of the building(s).
- Sections (depends on the size and complexity of the project).
- Perspective (not necessary but would help).
- Specification of materials to be used (this can be brief and not too technical).

## 3. Market research

Market research by a research company can at times prove to be very expensive and may only be necessary if the project is a reasonable size. Alternatively, you can conduct your own research. This can be achieved by seeking information from:
- Real estate agents active in the area to be developed.
- Valuers knowledgeable in the specified field.
- The Australian Bureau of Statistics.
- The Valuer General's office.
- The Housing Industry of Australia.
- The Property Council of Australia.
- Real estate journals, newspapers, and magazines.

The contents in the market research should cover data needed to endorse the proposed project. The following is necessary:
- Customer profile.
- Population demographics.
- Competition.
- Type of product.
- Pricing structure – existing and future.
- Promotional material required.

## 4. Development cost

You and your quantity surveyor or building estimator would have to spend a reasonable amount of time on this section, as it is one of the most important aspects of the study. It is also an area where the architect/designer will have to revise their plans to suit realistic budgets. Areas to be covered are:

o   *Land costs*

Land costs are made up of the cost of the present value of the land plus additional fees and charges such as stamp duty and conveyancing fees. In addition, other land expenses such as council rates, water rates and land tax, which are payable during the development period should be considered.

o   *Construction costs*

Construction costs can be reasonably calculated with a certain amount of accuracy by the measurement of the gross building areas and the application of a cost per square metre based on various forms of cost breakdowns for buildings of a similar nature that have been recently completed. The total cost should be adjusted for the rise and fall in both labour and material costs. These adjustments can be assessed by means of published construction indices, which have the concurrence of the building industry. Included under this category would be all professional fees and disbursements employed on the project.

o   *Finance costs*
These include all fees and charges and the interest on capital employed capitalised with the cash flow of the building pro-gramme of the development. Capital employed is broken into both debt and equity. Debt capital is money borrowed, usually from a financial institution, which accrues interest according to the various stages of the project when capital is required. Equity capital is the money provided by the developer as a "deposit" which should be shown as accrued interest. Although actual interest will not be incurred, an opportunity costs should be allowed for. Equity capital is generally expended before debt capital is advanced. Under this section the matured costs of leasing and sales fees should be also considered.

o   *Goods and Services Tax (GST)*
The effect of GST should be factored into the development and adjusted for cash flow.

## 5. Programme

A programme showing the development process together with the various stages from the inception of the idea to the comple-tion of the construction will assist you to formulate capital input and, more importantly, cash flow over the period of the project.

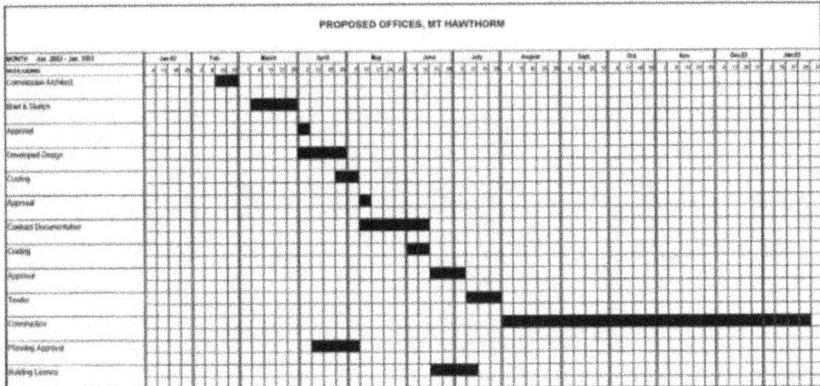

Diagram 8.1 Critical path analysis

## 6. Financial analysis

The purpose of financial analysis is to establish the expected return on the development. The development programme and the timing of cash flow are of importance, as they will affect the profitability of the project. Most developments will only see their income at the end of the project, so the bigger the project, the longer the programme and the more important is the timing of the cash flow.

As part of the financial analysis a sensitivity analysis should be brought into play, as this will give the worst- and best-case scenarios of the project. This is a "what if ..." exercise and the main variables that you should consider are:
- Land price.
- Construction cost.
- Pricing of sales.
- Holding cost.

A method that can be used to assess the sensitivity of the development is to adjust the above variables by a percentage, usually 10 per cent, and then recalculate the profitability or an internal rate of return (IRR), whichever is appropriate. The results should be graphed to indicate the sensitivity of the project. Below is an example illustration of such a graph.

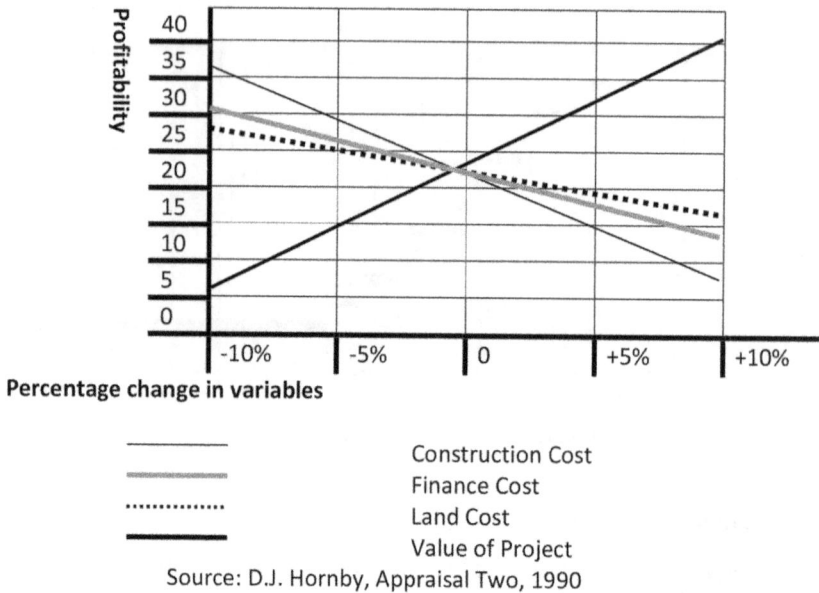

**Percentage change in variables**

| | |
|---|---|
| ——————— | Construction Cost |
| ~~~~~~~~~~~~ | Finance Cost |
| ················ | Land Cost |
| ——————— | Value of Project |

Source: D.J. Hornby, Appraisal Two, 1990

Figure 5.2

The above example indicates the sensitivity of changes to a development and the effect it has on its future value. By being aware of the elements that are most sensitive to changes, you can pay more attention to them to ensure that the project remains viable.

## 7. Real estate valuation

A sworn valuation by a credited and licensed property valuer will give your financiers confidence in the project. The fee for the valuation can vary according to the amount of work that has to be completed by the valuer. Depending on the size of the project and the amount of finance, investors or syndication you are trying to attract, an appraisal by the valuer of the property in its present format and one at completion would certainly be more favourable to the would-be financier or investor.

## 8. Marketing strategy

This would obviously be dependent upon your personal strategy and whether you are developing for rental or for sale. Whatever the case, you and your team should plan a marketing strategy that can be undertaken in conjunction with your marketing and advertising consultants. Under this section a concise description and budget for the marketing campaign should be explained. This should include:

- The marketing team.
- Budget estimates.
- Analysis of the current market situation.
- A clear definition of the marketing objectives.
- The position and differentiation of the development in relation to competitors.
- The market selection ensuring that there is a demand for such a development.
- The setting out of the plan of your marketing mix.
- Identification of critical success factors.
- Definition of a measurement system or checking system to see if the marketing plan is working.

## 9. Recommendation

This is an executive summary of the development and the possible returns expected from the project together with the recommendation on the actions that will be undertaken by you and your team. This section should include:

- An analysis of the risk involved.
- An analysis of the finance available.

## 10. Developer's financials

This information is only required if you are applying for finance and the aim is to prove your creditworthiness. Items to be included are the development company's or personal balance sheets, any additional assets to back the project and any reference from other lending institutions or other traders to prove credibility. Financial lenders would require the latest information and financials, which your accountant would be able to provide. Old financial records would not be of any use as the lender would not be able to make a proper assessment and recommendation.

## 11. Developer's credentials

This is basically your curriculum vitae and would be required if you intend to sell the project. In addition, it would assist with the application for finance. The information should prove your credibility and capacity to undertake the development. Although the histories of past developments are good endorsements, they are not as critical as your past management and business skills. Business and career references are helpful, but it is not necessary to include your junior scholastic or sporting achievements.

## 12. Presentation

As your feasibility may be viewed by several people including the management of the lending authority, your document must look impressive and professional. Enclose all the above research and information in a bound folder, preferably in an A4 format. Add colour graphics and colour photographs as this always creates a lasting impression. If your document is quite comprehensive, a contents list at the beginning referring to numbered pages will assist the reader to find specific information.

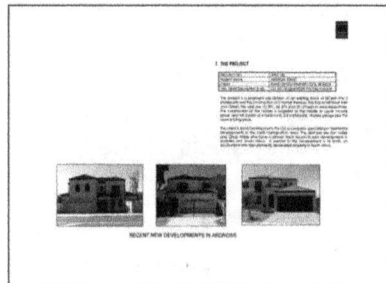

# Conclusion

In trying to determine if a development is worth the trouble, review the various factors and approaches relative to the type of property. In addition, review your personal return requirements, projected length of involvement in the project, your personal time required to create this potential profit, the risk associated with this particular type of development and any personal guarantees you may have to make. If the opportunity arises to develop more than one property, determine which development will be more successful.

# Chapter 9

# SELECTING THE RIGHT FINANCE OPTIONS

## Introduction

The procurement of equity and debt finance for a development is one of the most critical aspects of real estate development. Due to the high cost of development, few individuals have the means to finance a project themselves. Creative and lateral thinking is an essential and integral part of the funding of a development project.

Traditionally, real estate developers commit little of their capital to the long-term or permanent financing of their developments. They provide the start-up money or equity, which is then replaced with other sources of funding as the project develops. Real estate developers are entrepreneurs; they are the people with the vision and ideas but are not necessarily the financial contributors. These entrepreneurs provide the concept, time, effort, expertise and knowledge, as opposed to cash, for a project. As a result, financing is required in virtually all real estate development projects.

The ability of financial institutions to lend depends upon the inflow of deposits and the rate of repayments on outstanding mortgages. In 1983 the federal government deregulated Australia's financial system. Since then, we have seen the establishment of many new banks, several bank mergers, building societies becoming banks, industry superannuation funds offering loans and insurance companies entering the mortgage market. This increase in competition has been of great benefit to the consumer because loans have become more accessible.

## Factors affecting finance

When analysing from a financial perspective whether to undertake a development or not, the following factors should be considered:
- the state of the economy (timing)
- the flow of the money supply (Reserve Bank)
- inflation
- interest rates
- the real rate of interest, which is the difference between the Reserve Bank's prime interest rate and the inflation rate.

As discussed, the increase in interest rates usually leads to an increase in capitalisation rates, which in turn causes a reduction in market values. It mainly affects commercial real estate. During periods when market rentals escalate faster than building costs, it becomes more viable for the developer to enter the development market.

The abundance of loan products available and the aggressive marketing campaigns carried out by lending institutions often lead to uncertainty amongst borrowers. Therefore, when considering the options offered, a developer must not only look at the interest rate charged but also at the establishment fees, annual administration charges, early repayment penalties and the cost of refinancing arrangements if required. By shopping around, you can be sure of obtaining the best financial package to suit your development.

## The finance process

Before approaching a lender, be sure of the type of finance you are looking for by considering the following factors:
- Whether short-, medium- or long-term finance will be used. Short-term finance is usually granted for no longer than three years. Medium-term finance is generally granted for a period of three to seven years, and long-term finance is granted for periods above seven years.
- Which institutions are involved in financing the specific type of development you are proposing (for example, commercial banks or private lenders).
- The principal means of financing the development (for

example, mortgage or bridging finance) and what gearing opportunities are available to increase the return of the development.
- Whether alternative means of financing are available (for example, joint venture, syndications or trusts).

Lending institutions differ tremendously with regards to their policies and practices. Lender A might not even consider one type of proposal, while to Lender B, the same development is acceptable. Your success will depend upon your understanding of the various lending institutions' policies, practices and procedures, and the numerous options that are available in the finance industry.

## Costs and charges of raising finance

In addition to the developer's equity (deposit) required for a loan, there are several other costs — which are generally negotiable — that must be considered. These are:
- Bank fees and charges — including loan application fees, valuation fees, mortgage insurance and legal fees.
- Government fees — including stamp duty, registration fees, conveyancing fees, settlement fees, shire inquiry fees, water inquiry fees, land tax and disbursements.
- Raising fee (if required) — this is a fee of approximately two per cent, which is often charged when money is in short supply.

## Major sources of development finance

There are several major sources of funding for real estate developments. These include the following.

### Commercial banks

Commercial banks are mainly national institutions that are regulated by the Reserve Bank. These commercial banks specialise in predominantly short-term commercial credit, placing more emphasis on liquidity rather than savings, and they tend to be more conservative in their appraisals. One of the primary forms of short-term finance is the overdraft facility; however, several banks have become more involved in real estate financing through various subsidiaries.

Major commercial banks in Australia include the National Australia Bank (NAB), the Commonwealth Bank of Australia (CBA), Westpac Banking Corporation and the Australia and New Zealand Banking Group (ANZ).

## Savings banks

Credit unions, mutual building societies and mutual banks have a mutual structure, and their first point of business is to focus on their members (customers). Anyone can join and become a member. Each member of a credit union, mutual building society and mutual bank owns the organisation they belong to and have a vote in the organisation's governance.

These banks provide finance mainly through their depositors. The operation and involvement of general banks in real estate finance are like that of institutions previously known as building societies. The conversion of leading building societies into banks has been seen over the past number of years. The proportion of total home lending provided by building societies has declined. As a result, a number of these societies have merged operations as well as diversifying into insurance, advisory services and commercial financing. These banks are mainly involved in residential real estate mortgages and suburban development.

## Finance companies

The majority of finance companies lend money for real estate development rather than provide mortgage finance for homeownership. Most finance companies will advance up to 70 per cent of a development's value. It is wise to shop around for finance, however. When dealing with finance companies, be careful of the interest rates offered as they may charge 1.5 to 3.5 per cent above the variable rate.

## Mortgage managers

Mortgage managers are lending specialists who arrange funding for home and investment loans. Their role is to set up the loan and perform a liaison role with all parties involved — the originators, trustees, credit assessors and borrowers. Mortgage managers provide a customer service role and manage your loan throughout its term. They do not own the mortgage you take out with them. The original provider of the funds — a superannuation fund, unit trust or an individual — is the ultimate owner.

### Finance brokers

With the vast range of finance products on the market, it takes time to shop around for the best package to suit your development needs. As a result, several brokerage companies have arisen to assist the consumer. Finance brokers act as intermediaries and are responsible for introducing borrowers to lenders. The task of the finance broker is to determine the most suitable loan for the borrower. Although the broking service is generally free, a small fee may be charged, and the broker will usually receive a commission from the lender they recommend. However, be careful as brokers have financial arrangements with specific lenders who pay them a better commission.

## Methods of raising finance

Some standard methods of raising finance are discussed below.

### Mortgage bond

A mortgage bond may be defined as a loan to a third party which is endorsed on the title deed of a particular property where the property is being held as security for a debt of the property's owner. For a development project, there may be three levels of a mortgage bond, namely (a) land acquisition, (b) construction and (c) long-term investment.

- Land acquisition loan - is used to secure the purchase of raw land or a potential development site. Banks prefer not providing this as there is no income during the holding period.
- Construction loan - generally operates as an interest-only, drawdown facility to finance the building as required. Often the interest on a construction loan is capitalised during the building period.

- Long-term loan – when the building is complete and being rented out a longer-term mortgage loan is taken out over an extended period.

## Equity

Equity is usually the cash at-risk from either the developer or his partners, which bridges the gap between the lender's loan and the total costs of the development. It is also the value remaining in the property after payment of all debt or other charges on the property. An owner's equity in a property is usually the monetary interest the owner retains over and above the mortgage debt. If the property is encumbered with a long-term mortgage, the developer's equity in the property increases with each monthly principal mortgage payment, not including the increased value through appreciation.

## Bridging loans

Bridging loans are often used to quickly close on a property or take advantage of a short-term opportunity to secure long-term financing. Bridging loans on a property are typically paid back when the property is sold or refinanced with a traditional lender. It can also be when the borrower's creditworthiness improves, the property is improved or completed, or there is a specific improvement or change that allows a permanent or subsequent round of mortgage financing to occur. A bridging loan is often obtained by developers to carry a project while planning approval is sought. Because there is no guarantee the project will happen, the loan might be at a high-interest rate and from a specialised lending source that will accept the risk. Once the project is approved, a construction loan would then be obtained to take out the bridging loan and fund completion of the project.

## Mezzanine loans

Mezzanine loans are debt capital that gives the lender the rights to convert to an ownership or equity interest in the company if the loan is not paid back in time and in full. It is generally subordinated debt provided by private lenders or venture capital companies. This type of loan is advantageous because it is treated like equity and may make it easier to obtain standard bank financing. Mezzanine loans are often used by developers to secure additional funding for development projects where there is a shortfall of equity required by the senior lender.

Mezzanine loans are often a more expensive financing source for a developer than secured debt or senior debt. The higher cost of capital associated with mezzanine financings is the result of it being an unsecured, subordinated (or junior) debt in a project's capital structure. It means that in the event of default, the mezzanine financing is only repaid after all senior obligations have been satisfied. In compensation for the increased risk, mezzanine debt holders require a higher return for their money than secured or more senior lenders. This type of financing is aggressively priced with the lender seeking a return in the 20-30% range.

## Shares

Shares in companies are often sold on the stock exchange when a company decides to "list" or "float" itself. It is especially true of large syndicates, which hold diverse interests and are too large to raise additional finance through their members. Should a company wish to issue shares, the company does not need to list on the stock exchange, although larger companies often do. Share prices of listed companies fluctuate according to market forces to the advantage, and often, disadvantage, of the investor.

## Syndications

Syndications offer private investors participation in quality properties by way of real estate syndication memberships that combine the best features of real estate ownership with reduced risk. As investment or development into real estate syndication will only allow the purchaser ownership of a particular property and not a spread over a range of different properties, the risk is higher than investing into a real estate trust, for example.

The investment can be made through several legal structures such as partnerships, incorporated joint ventures or a unit trust structure, although schemes complying with the Managed Investments Act must be offered through a trust structure. The syndicate usually has a specified term of around 5 to 10 years, after which the property is sold, and the net proceeds returned to the investors. Syndicates can be broken into two categories, namely:

- *Private syndicates* — under this syndication a small group of individuals, perhaps friends or business associates, band together to buy and develop a property.
- *Public syndicates* — most offers to the public will require the promoter or manager to prepare and lodge a prospectus or information memorandum with ASIC. The prospectus sets out detailed information about the syndicate and the risks and expected returns relating to the investment. The syndicate may be promoted to the general public through licensed securities dealers, property managers, financial planners and accountants.

## Offshore finance

Offshore money is often sought in times of high-interest rates, similar to those experienced in the early 1990s. Interest rates abroad were comparatively low; however, investors often required additional security in the form of "forward cover", which is an additional cost on the rate of interest to cover the lending institution or investor against any currency fluctuations that may occur. Due to the long-term nature of real estate financing and instability caused by currency fluctuations, overseas financiers are reluctant to go abroad.

## Joint venture arrangements

An alternative means of financing a development project is a joint venture agreement. Often lenders may not be willing to lend money at low yields, but they may be willing to "joint venture" with the developer. The form of such joint ventures can vary according to the project. Some lenders may enter into a partnership and fund the purchase of the land and finance the development cost in return for a portion of the profits. Other lenders may buy the land and sign a contract with the developer for his services and parcel out the potential profits to the developer. Either way, the developer has been allowed to employ his skills with other people's money.

## How a lender assesses a loan

Lending institutions are conservative by nature and typically establish rigid lending policies. With most lenders, a loan policy committee determines the loan parameters, which include real estate types, locations and loan amounts. This committee will meet on a periodical basis to discuss its loan policy, review any problem loans and approve or disapprove new loan applications.

Before submitting a loan application to the committee, the loan officer will have carefully screened the borrower's creditworthiness, track record and credibility, completed an independent valuation on the development, reviewed the structure of the deal and made specific recommendations.

After the lender reviews and approves the loan, it will formulate the loan's terms and conditions. In setting the approval, the lender will consider the terms and conditions being offered by competing institutions, together with the risks associated with the development. These risks can include the type of project, the standard of tenants and the future income streams to repay the loan, as well as the financial strength of the developer and his or her track record. Listed below are the main areas of concern with regards to a development loan.

### Interest rate

Interest rates are based on the cost of money, and therefore the lender will review the cost of funds and calculate a desirable profit margin on these funds. The profit margin is based on the risk, the period for which these funds will be outstanding and the repayment schedule. A reduction in the rate may be considered if the developer is a good customer and has a distinguished track record.

### Loan fees and charges

Besides the interest rate, the lender will charge the developer a fee for organising the funds, as well as an annual ongoing service fee. Carefully scrutinise these fees as some low-interest rates offered initially are made up for in the various fees and charges. Also, note that very often a fee is charged for unused facilities.

## Loan period

Unless stipulated by the developer, the lender will determine the amount of time the borrower will have in which to repay the loan. The period will be based on several issues, such as the type of development and type of entity the developer is using.

## Financial guarantees

Besides the equity in the property to be developed, most lenders will require full or partial guarantees or sureties on a loan. You should try to reduce these financial guarantees as much as possible. Many developers have lost their fortunes because they made personal guarantees on developments that failed. One of the methods to reduce guarantees is to find a substitute or additional guarantors, but in using this method, the developer may have to share ownership of the development. Alternatively, the developer should increase the equity or deposit in the development and negotiate a guarantee for only the upper portion of the loan balance.

# Negotiating for a loan

After you have completed your feasibility study, and once you have decided which institution you will be approaching, complete the required application documents and submit them along with your feasibility study. Advise the lending officer that you are looking at other institutions. As I've mentioned, your feasibility study is an important document, and it should be well presented and researched because the lending officer is not the one who will make the necessary approval. It could quite possibly be the responsibility of a board of directors or committee who will not have met you and to whom you will not have the opportunity to present your development in person.

If the best one or two institutions approve your loan, review and analyse each loan offer, as each institution will be different, after you have decided which of the offers is the best, request a written confirmation and commitment. Some lenders may require a non-refundable commitment fee to be paid upon acceptance. At this stage, you should request a copy so that your solicitor can examine the documents. You and your solicitor should take special care in assessing your obligations. Most finance documents are prepared in favour of the lender, and many clauses will not be ne-gotiable but can be reworded to benefit the developer. It is more common to negotiate these clauses in commercial transactions than in housing loans.

When viewing your loan, look at all the options and be creative in your thinking. There are many options for refining the loan to meet your needs. Each party to a loan transaction has its criteria, and with good, creative thinking each can reach its objectives. Remember that lenders are in the business to make money and do so by lending money. Therefore, if one proposal is not suitable, look for another that will satisfy both parties. Your accountant or attorney could also assist in this regard.

## Conclusion

To find and secure financing, the developer must understand how to identify potential lenders, present the financing proposal, and negotiate and close the loan. When searching for the perfect loan, I always try to negotiate with more than one lender at a time. I identify several available lending institutions and consider them all. I have found that, even though the loan officer has informed me that my application appears to be acceptable, the terms change entirely by the time the loan committee approves the finance. Since time is of the essence, negotiating with more than one lender could be to your advantage. Also, when submit-ting your loan proposal, ensure that it is complete and that all relevant details have been included. It will decrease the loan pro-cessing time and increase your chances of having the application approved.

# Chapter 10

# *MANAGING YOUR WAY TO SUCCESS*

## Introduction

Developing real estate is undoubtedly one of the most complex businesses around, and the key to a successful development project is its effective and responsible management and, more specifically, the management of the people involved. The real estate development industry encompasses a diverse range of people, from professionals to government bureaucrats, and from contractors to building material suppliers.

Daily, a real estate developer is constantly surrounded by people from all walks of life with whom he or she has to manage. These people may include the official from the Council's planning department to the carpet-layer on the construction site. Experienced developers understand that it is virtually impossible for one person to handle all these people at the same time and have consequently learnt the art of delegation as well as good management and leadership skills. If you sense that you do not have the skills or the personal time available to manage the project, you should appoint an experienced development manager or project manager to perform the management duties on your behalf.

## The role of the developer

The role of the developer is pivotal in all real estate developments. Any form of inefficiency on their part, or failure to adhere to the basic principles of management, can result in unnecessary financial losses. Figure 10.1 is a simple diagram showing the position of the developer at the centre and the various members of the development team and entities that the developer must deal with during the development process.

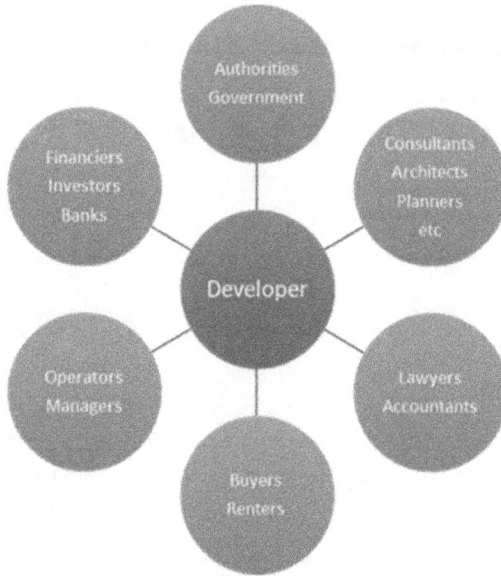

Figure 10.1 Role of a developer

A developer should ensure that everyone involved is working well together, that decisions are made promptly to keep the project on track. That expenditure is controlled to maintain the project budget (unless some agreement is made to increase this amount through a change in content or quality). Written records of all agreements influencing the building contract should always be kept in a safe filing system.

## Dealing with and managing people

The developer must be able to manage and deal with a wide range of people effectively. Below are some tips on how to undertake these tasks.

### Delegating

How you delegate, and how much you delegate, involves great skill, self-control and astute judgement. Nobody can delegate appropriately without understanding the theory that you don't buy a dog and then do the barking yourself. Therefore, when you instruct somebody to do a job, you must ensure that you:

- define the job clearly
- ask the person how he or she proposes to carry out the task
- let the person get on with the job and report to you regularly.

## Negotiation

The negotiating process is one of communicating with others as a means of obtaining what you want from them. The main goal of negotiating is to reach an agreement in which both parties feel that they have benefited. Three ingredients are vital in every negotiation, and the successful negotiator will always use them. These are:

1. information — gathering of information on the other party or subject
2. time — the handling of time constraints
3. control — keeping emotions under control and focusing on the bottom line.

When negotiating, there are specific points to consider. Some of them are described below.

*Look for a win-win situation.*

The best result in any negotiation is a situation where both parties feel that they have achieved their objective with their dignity and integrity intact. The secret to understanding the win-win concept is to find out the other party's motivation. It proves that having information is vital.

*Price is not always important.*

Many negotiating deals fall flat because both or one of the parties believe that the lowest price will seal the deal. Look at the terms and conditions of the deal, as there may be mitigating factors that may affect the price in the medium term.

*A third party is helpful.*

During a face-to-face negotiation, there may be times when you are forced into a position where you are unable to compromise. Therefore, it is always better to have an absent third party such as a business partner, a board of directors, or a consultant to use as a negotiating lever. It will allow you to delay your decision without jeopardising the position or embarrassing either party.

*Look at all options*

Quite often in a negotiation, one party is preoccupied with one particular issue at the expense of others. It is human nature that everybody likes to win but the more options that one has on the negotiating table, the better it is for all concerned.

*Control your emotions*

When the stakes are high, negotiations can reach a point where emotions come into play. During this period, the egos of both parties should not get in the way of finalising the deal. When this occurs, it is best to take time out and rethink the issues at hand or devise alternative strategies.

*Split the difference*

When all the solutions have been exhausted, one of the better solutions is to split the difference. It may not be determined purely by price as conditions can also influence negotiation outcomes. Remember, the art of compromise is that you may have to give in to one point to gain a more valuable one!

*Walk away*

If you feel uncomfortable with the way negotiations are heading and that the other party is not budging at all, walk away from the deal, as there will always be another opportunity around the corner.

## Basic principles of good management

There are many books on management, and it is advisable to read these and, if necessary, take a short course on the subject. Below are the main management principles applicable to real estate development:

- Focus on results, namely what to achieve and how to achieve it in a specified timeframe.

- Always be in control of what is happening on your project, especially problems, even though they may be minor. It is best to resolve a fault before it festers and develops into a major issue which can cause delays and waste money.
- Make effective and timely decisions. Every person under your wing is waiting for your instruction on the next stage of the development or your resolution to a problem. If you are still a novice in this area and not knowledgeable about technical issues, it is at times best to ask the people involved for suggestions and select the best solution.
- Ensure that all finances, budgets and construction are kept in order. An astute developer will also employ efficient consultants and reprimand those who do not perform their tasks diligently.
- Ensure that you or your staff keep and file all records, minutes, correspondence and invoices in an orderly fashion.
- Read the fine print in every document and ask questions if you are uncertain about a specific point.
- Organise your daily activities in an orderly manner and do not be late for an appointment or meeting. If you are running late, it is good manners to inform the other party. It creates a wrong impression if you are consistently late. It shows signs of inefficiency.
- Confirm any verbal agreement or discussion in writing. These documents will be vital if a problem arises during the development.

## Dealing with your professional team

A developer relies heavily on the expertise and professional advice of the development team. Extracting the best information and motivating them to do the best on your project will depend on how you manage them. Some pointers for effectively managing a team are as follows:
- Show leadership qualities and gain the respect of your consultants by being firm and fair.
- Give members of your team guidance and set clear goals for the project.
- Be tactfully severe to consultants who do not perform their duties diligently and professionally.

- Be positive and enthusiastic about your project. This way, consultants will feel more comfortable, especially if they are working at risk.
- Be approachable and compliment consultants for any diligent performance.
- Confirm any contractors' appointments if the consultant fails to do so.

## Guidelines for meetings

During a development project, there is an astonishing number of meetings with the consulting team, council officials, builders and subcontractors. Much time can be wasted if the purpose of the meeting, and items to be discussed are not clearly defined before the meeting takes place. Therefore, it is essential to provide your team with a comprehensive agenda before the meeting. A sample agenda (Figure 10.2) is provided below.

All attendees must share a common understanding of the goals of the meeting and what is to be achieved by the end. When meeting with consultants, it is vital that the team fully understands the aim of the project, including the scope, budgets and, importantly, the timeframes and deadlines. All discussions must end with a schedule of actions to be undertaken by specific people to prevent any misunderstanding or delays.

Rules for meetings should be given at the beginning, and the chairperson should advise attendees accordingly. Some essential rules are:

- Time of the meeting — it is essential to be firm with late arrivals and non-attendees who do not submit apologies for not being present.
- Leadership role — it must be communicated in the meeting that you will act as captain of the group and, as such, your instructions should be solely in the interest of the project.
- Responsibility for actions — attendees must be accountable for not carrying out designated activities.
- Length of the meeting — do not allow anyone to continue with the discussion that does not pertain to the subject of the meeting.
- Mobile telephones — all mobile phones should be switched

off during meetings. If attendees need to take a call, they should be excused from the meeting to do so.

## Agenda: management meetings

The following agenda is only a guide and should be amended as the need arises. The context should, however, remain the same.

1.  Welcome
2.  Apologies
3.  Confirmation of previous minutes
4.  Matters arising from previous minutes
5.  Progress report and action
    a.  Client
    b.  Town planner
    c.  Architect
    d.  Quantity surveyor
    e.  Structural engineer
    f.  Civil engineer
    g.  Mechanical/electrical engineer
    h.  Other: legal advisors, etc.
6.  Tenant report by broker
7.  Report on finance
8.  General
9.  Date of next meeting
10. Schedule of meetings

# Dealing with government authorities

When dealing with government officials, bear in mind that they work to rules and guidelines which are different from your own and often not with the same sense of urgency. It is mainly due to the stringent structure and red tape that exists in the system. Developers should take time to learn about development procedures within the local government organisation, and this will hopefully result in them becoming less frustrated. Local councils and other bodies controlling building and development are interested in three things: health, safety and amenity. They can also be exposed to public outcry or being sued for approving poor developments.

The pressure of modern urban life has created regulations

aimed at ensuring the health and safety of building users. Far more contentious to developers are the extensive discretionary powers used by the authorities to control the aesthetic quality and zoning of developments, and this can lead to confrontation. If you believe you are within your rights and have the time and resources to do so, there are two possible grounds of appeal. These include the merits of the proposal or that the council did not properly carry out its administrative function when making its decision.

Although there are the national building regulations, individual councils may have their interpretations or their own established by-laws. At times, officials in the same department may have a different understanding of a particular rule. It is essential that when an official gives an interpretation, you make sure that you have his or her name and a written confirmation of the official's interpretation.

One of the better ways to deal with government authorities, especially with the local council's planning services, is to have a preliminary meeting about your project before you put pen to paper. Ask them for their guidance as it will make them feel part of the project. It will also give them a sense of what you are trying to achieve and how they could support your proposal. It is a strategy that has worked favourably for my clients and me over the many projects.

## Dealing with buyers

If you are developing to sell your project, whether a speculative single-family home, a block of apartment units to be sold to the general public or a shopping centre to be sold to a major corporation, there are several factors you should be considered. These include being objective, knowing all the facts and figures about the development and being fully aware of your competition. These factors are described as follows.

### Be objective

Be objective about the property you are selling. Do not get personally involved as this may result in a situation whereby the property may be overpriced initially, and any negotiation may become emotional.

### Know what you are selling

It is imperative that whoever is selling the development has all the facts and figures at hand. It includes zoning, council rates and construction specifications. Failure to have full knowledge of the property may result in concessions being made.

### Avoid desperation

Be careful not to show any form of desperation or urgency. Astute buyers will seek a seller who is forced to sell and hold out and target the seller's rock-bottom price.

### Tricky buyers

Be aware of tricky buyers who arrange for a third party to approach you to test your selling position. Once found out, these buyers may use delaying tactics to reduce your bargaining position.

### Be aware of possible negatives.

Anticipate any negatives that will be brought out as a justification for bargaining concessions. Buyers may point out items such as the lack of surrounding amenities or the locality compared to your competitors.

### Know your competition

By knowing what your competitors are selling, you can be one step ahead with your marketing strategy. Buyers will always use a competitor's price as a bargaining tool.

### Set the correct price

Overpriced properties will not attract buyers, and prospective purchasers may wait until the price drops. If you have a real estate sales consultant selling on your behalf, you will find that they will not actively market your property until the price falls within the correct market range.

### Qualify buyers

By not screening buyers who cannot obtain necessary financing or who do not have the authority to act, you may waste a great deal of personal time and energy.

### Avoid concessions

Most real estate transactions will require a reasonable conces-
sion plan. However, avoid agreeing to too many concessions that
depend on the buyer's subjective whims. It can place you at the
mercy of the buyer.

### Scrutinise the offer

Carefully look at all aspects of an offer and ensure that it fits your
requirements. A cash offer may not be as attractive if unreasonable terms and conditions accompany it.

### Keep control

Maintain control of all conditions attached to an offer. Failure by
your conveyancer to be attentive to settlement dates and dates
by which conditions must be met may leave you out of control and
therefore losing time and money.

## Dealing with tenants

If you decide to hold and lease your development as a long-term
investment, there are management and administrative duties to
be performed. You have the choice of doing the management
yourself, thereby saving the agent's fees, or employing a competent property manager. The latter is often preferable as; otherwise,
it can become challenging to distance oneself from the property,
resulting in emotional involvement. Also, it will give you more time
to concentrate on your other developments. Whether you decide
to employ a property manager or not, you should consider the
following points to maximise your returns and minimise potential
problems.

### Tenant screening

The screening tenants aims to determine whether they will look
after your property and whether they can pay their rent. Requesting
a reference from a previous landlord is a good way of doing this.
Alternatively, if they have never rented before, a recommendation

from their employer should be obtained. Where possible, it is also wise to run a credit check through one of the recognised credit agencies.

## Leases

The type of lease will depend on the type of property. For residential real estate, there are several standard leases available from various institutions. With commercial real estate, a lawyer who is knowledgeable in the real estate field generally draws up the lease. A lease protects you, the landlord, and the tenant. In the case of residential real estate, a minimum occupation of six months is standard, whereas in commercial real estate, the longer the lease, the better, with a minimum of one year.

## Security bond

Part of a lease agreement is a property condition report, which is generally conducted by the tenant and the landlord or his or her agent. The report will outline the condition of the property at the start of the tenancy and includes any defects. A security bond is collected to cover any damage or further defects to the property at the end of the lease. This bond is usually a predetermined amount that may differ from State to State and according to other circumstances. In most instances, a security bond to the value of four to eight weeks' rent is set and, in most States, legislation requires the bond to be placed with a rental bond authority. Bonds are frequently a disputed area of a lease agreement, so they should be carefully and correctly defined in the lease agreement.

## Rent

Rent can be collected personally, delivered to you by mail or deposited directly into your bank account. It is one area where a property manager is handy, as tenants perceive that the manager has more power when it comes to rent collection. Managers are also unemotional when they must evict a tenant for failure to pay or any other breach of the lease agreement. The rent always should reflect the prevailing market rates. Ensure that there is an escalation clause in your lease agreement to cover the annual increase in cost.

## Inspections

Property inspections should be held at least every six months to alert you to any maintenance problems that may require attention and to see whether your tenant is treating your property with care. Also, it is wise that you drive past your property from time to time.

## Finding tenants

You can look for tenants yourself by doing your own advertising, or you could use the services of a real estate broker. By going it alone, you will probably advertise through the weekend papers or an internet marketing platform for tenants or place advertising signs on the property. By choosing this method, you will be faced with the job of screening each tenant and showing him or her the property, which can be quite time-consuming. If you decide to use an agent, he or she will do the necessary advertising and screening and will charge you a commission, which can be either an agreed fixed sum or a percentage based on the term of the lease.

## Relationship with tenants

Handle all your dealings with tenants professionally and courteously. Having a cordial but firm relationship with your tenant can solve possible problems before they get out of hand. Remember not to become emotionally involved with your tenants, as it may prove challenging to act firmly if they are falling behind with their rent.

## Maintenance

Although the property you are renting is new when your first tenants move in, you will still have to budget for future maintenance which requires a maintenance program. It is always easier to rent properties that are in good condition. There are four types of maintenance activities that will occur during the lifetime of the property:

1. Preventative — this involves a regular program of inspections of both the interior and exterior of the building, equipment and open ground. The aim is to eliminate any

future costly maintenance and preserve the integrity of the premises.

2. Corrective — this form of maintenance involves the replacement and repair of certain items that occur now and then and ensures that the property is in good working condition.
3. Routine — this is the general housekeeping of the property and includes the cleaning and the maintenance of the landscaped areas.
4. Emergency — this includes emergency repairs to leaking pipes and roofs, to broken air-conditioning units.

## Conclusion

The developer is generally seen as the project's figurehead by those working for him or her. Therefore, your leadership should be exemplary, your decision-making sound and management effective. Besides, do not tackle more than you can handle, especially if you do not know how to delegate or have a responsible back-up manager.

In a "real estate boom" period and when the market is buoyant, one can easily fall into the trap of taking on too many projects at the same time. I was once caught in this situation where I was developing three separate townhouse projects, two shopping centres and an entertainment centre at once. As matters progressed, I realised that some of the projects were on the brink of failure, simply because I did not have the time to pay them an equal amount of attention. Plus, I did not have appropriately trained managers on hand to take care of the neglected projects.

Therefore, be sure to know your limitations before biting off more than you can chew – assess whether you have the management ability or the correct management structure in place.

# Chapter 11

# SMALL RESIDENTIAL DEVELOPMENTS

## Introduction

Small residential developments, whether they are homes newly built for speculative reasons or renovated older homes for resale or a duplex development, are an ideal start for a novice developer. It is the best way to start to learn and gain experience in real estate development without risking a great deal financially. The four more popular developments are:

- the renovated, older 'character' home in an established suburb that may just require some repainting and maybe a new kitchen or an additional bedroom.
- the speculative new home (called speculative because the developer will not have an end buyer or tenant established from the outset, and therefore is taking on risk) is usually built on a single lot in a new land subdivision, or on an older block that has been subdivided into a smaller lot normally found in older suburbs
- a duplex or triplex residential development are ideal for developers who would like to build up a real estate portfolio where they can hold one home and sell the other(s), reduce debt and generate a passive income.
- Sub-division of an older property has become increasingly popular since the increase in zoning densities is some older suburbs which allows an owner to sub-divide their land and develop a new home at the rear.

## Benefits and risks

Below is a list of some of the key benefits and risks to consider when undertaking a small housing project.

### Benefits

Compared to larger commercial development or apartment projects, smaller residential developments provide the benefits listed below.

*Low initial investment*

Most homes require a smaller amount of capital to get started. Depending on your financial position, some lending institutions will not require a deposit (providing you can show another form of security). In contrast, others may need only 10 to 25 per cent of the total development cost to start. It allows you to leverage your financial position.

*Ease of financing*

Most lending institutions have the infrastructure and systems to make home loans easy for their applicants. With more banks and new mortgage companies entering the market, finance for a home is a lot easier to raise than for other forms of development.

*Favourable tax laws*

If you build a home, live in it for 12 months and then sell it, the profit made will not be subject to capital gains tax. Beware, though, that this will not always be the case if this is done frequently. If you retain the home as an investment and rent it out, you will be able to negatively gear the property, which means that the shortfall in interest payable on the mortgage loan is tax-deductible.

*Superior liquidity*

With finance more readily available, smaller housing developments are a lot easier to sell than other forms of development. Besides, there are generally not as many conditions attached to their sales, making settlement and sales procedures a lot faster.

### Market not as sophisticated

Buyers in this market are not as sophisticated as seasoned investors, who will generally negotiate tenaciously on several issues, thereby delaying any sale settlement or transfer of proceeds, and in turn affecting the developer's profit.

### Good capital growth

Housing prices fluctuate according to supply and demand. Quite often, during a boom period, housing prices peak, and this sets the benchmark for future prices. The capital growth, in this instance, can be quite significant. Prices on commercial buildings, on the other hand, are governed by the leases they have in hand.

## Risks

While smaller residential developments have traditionally been considered safe developments, there are still certain risks involved, including the following.

### Volatile market

I mentioned previously that the concept of herd mentality is relevant to the housing industry and that the boom and bust economic cycles have a significant impact on housing. In recessionary periods housing prices stagnate or fall significantly followed by price increase when the economy starts improving. Therefore, developers must be careful not to develop real estate at the peak of the boom but rather when the market is beginning to pick up.

### Strong competition

Smaller residential developments are a less complicated form of development and thus, is extremely popular. But even though there are many players in the game, there is still money to be made by the astute developer who stays one step ahead of the competition. In the past decade, I have noticed an increase in the number of new home developers, and most of them are new migrants. Given the rise in business migrants, it is no surprise that those with substantial cash often enter the real estate market.

*Inefficient use of land*

Plot ratios and densities set out by the local authorities on the traditional quarter-acre lot make the cost of land more expensive when compared to a higher density residential development.

# Market demand

The demand for smaller residential developments is affected by many factors, some of which are listed below.

### A high rate of homeownership

Despite the housing affordability problem in the cities like Sydney and Melbourne, Australia still has one of the highest rates of homeownership amongst the industrialised nations, and this fuels the demand for investment and development in housing. More than sixty per cent of Australian households owned or were buying a dwelling. Homeownership is an aspiration for many Australians and is widely referred to as 'the great Australian dream'. Homeownership also provides people with a financial asset from which they can benefit, especially in later life, when their earning potential has reduced.

### Population growth

The demand for single-family homes in Australia is ever increasing. Although we presently have a population of 25 million, we have one of the highest rates of homes per capita compared to other developed countries. According to the Australian Bureau of Statistics, Australia's population would reach 30 million in 2030-31, 35 million in 2043-44 and 40 million in 2058-59. By the year 2066, it would be 42 million.

### Family homes

While apartments seem to dominate the housing supply, very few buildings and new projects do not cater for growing families. Very few apartment buildings have three-bedroom units, and if they do, they are over-priced and not within financial reach for most families. It, therefore, creates an opportunity for small residential developers to fulfil this gap even though such opportunities are mainly found in the suburbs away from the CBD.

## Development strategies

When you develop a small residential development, you will be left with the dilemma of whether to sell or rent. Before making your choice, consider the following strategies.

### Build and sell

Most developers intend to sell so that they can reap the profits and continue to a new project. In pursuing this strategy, you must firstly look at the tax implications of the sale and, secondly, analyse your financial gearing (equity-to-debt ratio) so that you are not jeopardising your financial position if the market turns for the worst.

### Build and rent

If you intend to build and rent, ensure that you have the financial resources to follow this strategy. If you have borrowed money and your development is too highly geared, you could be caught if the market turns and interest rates escalate.

### Build, part sell and part rent.

If you do not have strong financial backing, an idea is to initially sell some of your early developments until you have built a reasonable equity base and then retain some of the later developments as income for your retirement.

### Which strategy?

Your feasibility studies and future projections will help you to decide which of these strategies to follow. Always look at your gearing position and work out the worst-case scenario. Depending on the viability of your project, some banks may allow you to borrow 80 per cent of the home's value, which invariably you will have to negatively gear. It is all well and good if have the income to sustain your investment. However, some conservative investors would only hold property on a 40:60 equity-to-debt ratio basis which is safer.

## Market profile

The market profile of a typical buyer or renter in this sector can be broken down into the following categories, depending on the buyer's or renter's preferences for specific amenities.

### A young couple with no plans for children

In the case of a young couple who have no plans for children, both parties are usually working and career-minded. Although this market is being catered for by apartment developments, this type of living may not be their cup of tea. As their lifestyles are hectic, they generally prefer a smaller garden with less maintenance. Parking facilities for two motor vehicles are attractive to these buyers.

### Young couple planning a family

Essential areas for a young couple planning a family are a good-sized kitchen, master bedroom suite, secondary rooms and an outside play area (possibly with space for a future pool). This category of buyers or renters prefer to be located near schools and decent shopping facilities.

### A single parent with children at home

The single parent with children still living at home prefer a family room, a master bedroom suite and secondary bedrooms. Locations near schools, community facilities and public transport facilities are preferred.

### Established family

A formal dining area, well-appointed kitchen, with the master bedroom suite separate from other secondary bedrooms, would generally suit the established family profile. Parking facilities for at least two vehicles and visitor bays are preferable.

### Professional established family

The executive husband and wife who have a respectable profile in the community, generally look for a home with a formal entry, formal dining, guestroom and study with good security and privacy. Preferable locations are the up-market areas.

## Location analysis

Before purchasing a property for your development, consider the following in terms of its locality:

- Commuting times and distances to important public amenities should be short.
- Public transport should be within walking distance.
- Shopping facilities should be close by and easily accessed.
- Recreational and cultural amenities should be of a good standard and easy to access.
- The quality and prestige of the community should suit your target market.

Also, weigh up the following factors:

- the quality and access to schools
- the local population's density
- the quality of community facilities and council services
- the level of crime in the area
- the availability of medical facilities.

## Site analysis

When selecting a building site for a small housing development, there are several investigations which should be completed before the purchase is made. You should ensure that the site:

- is free from the dangers of flooding that is associated with low lying, swampy areas, streams and watercourses.
- is not located near drainage catch-pit areas or drainage channels where there is a history of flooding.
- is not subject to soil settlement normally experienced with ex-rubbish tips or landfill areas — research the history of the site and do a soil analysis if necessary.
- is not adjacent to existing or future commercial or industrial activity — check the town-planning scheme with your local council.
- is accessible from a public street or, if the access street is private, make sure there is a maintenance agreement between all parties using the road.
- is not on a major arterial road as traffic noise and vehicular access and egress will be a major problem.

- is not in an area where there is a possibility of change of use — again, check with your local council about future planning changes for the area.
- is not restricted by zoning, building lines or any other building codes that may affect the design of the home — check with your local council.
- has a title which is not restricted by outstanding mortgages, easements or any other covenants such as native land title.
- has essential services such as water, electricity, gas, telephone and sewerage available.
- is not governed by any stringent planning codes, such as restrictions on the use of materials and setbacks if it is in a specially planned estate — check these conditions and make sure that they are not too onerous and costly.

## Market research

For a small housing development, extensive and expensive market research is not as important as it is for larger-scale developments. A comparable market analysis is useful for this purpose, as it is a breakdown of recent sales within a specific market area. The data compares several dwellings by size and type, location, and how much they sold for. Your local real estate agent, property valuer or online real estate platforms will be able to assist with this type of analysis.

### Previous sales

By listing the most recent sales in the area you intend to develop in, you will be able to ascertain what size of home you should be building and what price you will be able to realise. Also, analyse the history of appreciation in value for similar properties over the last few years and estimate the possible appreciation you could see in the future.

### Present rentals

Examining the present rentals in the area in which you wish to develop is essential, regardless of whether you are going to sell or rent. Even if your intention is to sell, you could be caught if the market turns and you are forced to rent. By analysing the present rentals, you will at least know what rental income is achievable so that you can structure your finances accordingly.

## Development team

Developing a smaller residential project does not require as many team members as a larger development; however, you should be honest with yourself and ask two essential questions:

1.  Do I have the time to manage this project?
2.  Do I have the technical expertise and knowledge to handle the building?

How much time and knowledge you have available will determine the level of service you will require from the following consultants.

### Architect or building designer

The architect or building designer can provide the full service from inception to completion or be employed on a partial basis. These consultants can provide design, building cost estimates, working drawings, tendering and supervision.

### Land surveyor

A land surveyor will be needed to provide a 'contour feature' survey indicating the various levels on the site, existing trees, existing services and street furniture such as streetlights, bus shelters and signposts. This information is vital to the architect as certain aspects may influence the design of the home.

### Building estimator

A building estimator is a qualified technician who can provide a spreadsheet showing the quantity of building materials, the cost of labour and a total estimated cost to build a new home or renovate an existing building. You will not require an estimator if your plans are being tendered to several builders; however, if you are building the development yourself, the services of an estimator will be necessary.

### Structural engineer

Depending on soil conditions and whether the home is double storey, the services of a structural engineer will be required.

## Prepare a building budget.

For your residential development to succeed, you must be very stringent with your development budget and ensure that you do not overcapitalise on the project. When briefing your designer, make sure that he or she is aware of the budget and, more importantly, what items are included in it. Remember that you are selling a completed home and, therefore, you must allow for all finishing items, including landscaping and fencing. Table 11.1 is a checklist and table for calculating your budget.

| ITEM | BUDGET | ACTUAL |
|------|--------|--------|
| 1.   Cost of land | | |
| 2.   Transfer cost | | |
| 3.   Finance cost | | |
| 4.   Construction budget | | |
| 5.   Professional fees | | |
| 6.   Siteworks | | |
| 7.   Fencing | | |
| 8.   Connection fees | | |
| 9.   Planning fees | | |
| 10.  Gas supply | | |
| 11.  Carport/garage | | |
| 12.  Paving | | |
| 13.  Verge crossover | | |
| 14.  Pergola | | |
| 15.  Landscaping | | |
| 16.  Reticulation | | |
| 17.  Painting | | |
| 18.  Floor finishes | | |
| 19.  Window treatments | | |
| 20.  Light fittings | | |
| 21.  Insulation | | |
| 22.  Other | | |
| TOTAL | | |

Table 11.1: Budget spreadsheet

The costs in your budget are estimates, and you should allow for the real building costs to be approximately five to ten per cent higher. It allows for contingencies and inflation of building costs by the time you start building. When it comes to these calculations, it is best to be conservative as any budget blow out will be a setback.

## Design considerations

Having analysed the above, you will now be able to brief your designer on the type of home you intend to develop. Listed below are some additional design considerations that can be included in the brief.

### Street appeal

First impressions are essential to any potential buyer or renter. Spending money on good aesthetics, including an interesting architectural character and a well-presented, landscaped front garden will help you sell or rent the home.

### Lightness and brightness

With today's escalating building cost and reduced budgets, builders and developers are building homes with smaller spaces. A trick to make a room look larger is to incorporate bigger windows that will introduce additional natural light.

### Open plan living

Open-plan living is becoming more desirable. Designing rooms that flow into each other not only makes spaces look bigger but also provides an appealing aesthetic.

### Solar design

Because of our extreme temperatures in Australia, it is wise to design the home with the right solar aspect. Also, buyers are becoming more aware of the importance of good solar design.

## Wasted space

Planning rooms around the furniture that will be used, as well as incorporating practical dimensions and reducing passages like lengthy corridors will decrease wasted space and therefore reduce the cost of the building.

## Security

Secure access from the garage or carport directly into the home is attractive to most buyers. This access is not only a security feature, but it is also convenient, especially after grocery shopping.

Figure 11.1 below is a drawing of a typical four-bedroom family home that can be found in most new Australian suburbs. Notice that it incorporates many of the design considerations listed above.

Figure 11.1: Sample plan

## Building contract

Depending on the size and scale of your project and your pre-set budget, the usual contract adopted by most builders is the fixed-price contract. In any fixed-price contracts, try to avoid variations as they will not only delay the construction period but will increase your budget. Make sure that all warranties are in place and that there is a maintenance contract covering the period following the completion of the home. Also, ensure that the builder is not requesting a higher deposit than the legal limit and only pay a claim after been vetted by a third party such as your bank or your architect if you have appointed one to undertake the supervision of the contract.

## Construction stage

Although the construction of a small residential development is not complicated compared to larger projects, it is essential that you or your architect supervise the work. It is to ensure that the works are executed correctly, according to an agreed program, and to the contract documentation and specifications. On a standard single storey, there are basically five stages of construction. These are:

1. Slab down — this is the stage where the concrete ground floor slab has been completed, together with any brick build-up, under-slab services or electrical wiring that may be required.
2. Plate height — this is the stage where all brickwork or framework, including both internal and external walls, has been completed. Door- and window frames are usually built-in at this stage.
3. Roof cover — at this stage, roof framing or roof trusses and the roof cover, as well as gutters and downpipes, are installed.
4. Lock-up — by this stage, windows have been glazed, doors and locks have been fitted, the electrical and plumbing 'rough-in' has been completed, the ceilings have been installed, finishing carpentry is installed and plastering completed.

5. Completion — this stage signifies the completion of all finishing items, such as cabinetwork, sanitary and plumbing work, electrical switches and light fittings, painting, tiling and floor finishes.

Some financial institutions would use the above stages as a guide to making various progress payments to the builder. For example, after each stage, a building inspector from the financial institution will inspect the construction and determine if the claim for payment submitted by the builder is justified.

## Construction alternatives

The above process explains the conventional way to develop your small residential project. There are two alternatives to the process, and these are listed below.

### Owner–building

Owner–building done correctly will save money; however, it is not recommended unless you have enough technical knowledge of the building process and time to manage the project.

### Project building

Appointing a project builder to build for you could save you both time and money if you select plans off their shelves and keep the variations to the plans and specifications to an absolute minimum.

## Marketing

The marketing of residential real estate can either be done by you or by your local real estate agent who will undertake all the necessary marketing and advertising. In doing it yourself, you save money by not paying a commission, but you should account for the following costs:
- preparation of a brochure of the development
- advertisements in the local newspaper and various real estate journals
- signage on the property.

If you decide to use the services of a local real estate agency, you will benefit from numerous services, including assistance in pricing the property, showing the property, investigating sources of finance and closing the sale. It also provides an independent barrier between the buyer and the developer, who may be emotionally attached to his or her building. If you do decide to employ a reputable sales agent, consider the following factors.

### Should the agent be given an exclusive?

Most agents would naturally prefer an exclusive right to sell the property they list. This right is only justified if the agent will actively market the development and has the available resources to provide the right service. Developers should carefully assess the agent's capabilities before granting an exclusive listing.

### Has the agent defined the services which will be provided?

The marketing of property involves several issues besides advertising, and these include holding open inspections, dealing with buyers and their representatives and ensuring that relevant legal documents are issued to various parties. The seller's agreement should define the steps the agent will take to promote the property.

### Has the agent explained the terms and conditions?

Agent's agreements may contain automatic continuation clauses or clauses to the effect that commissions may be due before the completion of the sale. The agreement should fully explain when commissions are expected, the agreed commission percentage and when the agency agreement or listing terminates.

## Conclusion

If you are a novice and want to gain some experience in real estate development, buy a block of land, get a home designed, contract a builder and then sell it at a profit. Only by taking the initiative and starting with a small development will you be able to get an insight into this industry. Whether you make a large or small profit on your first small residential development is not that crucial. Tthe vital issue is that you gain invaluable experience so that your next development is a more significant success.

# Chapter 12

# HIGHER DENSITY RESIDENTIAL DEVELOPMENTS

## Introduction

Traditionally, Australians dream of building and owning a home on a quarter-acre lot. In more recent times, these visions have changed due to several factors. These include:
- affordability
- practicality
- the changing demographic distribution of our population
- the changing structures in household formations.

These factors have created a demand for more diversified types of housing, including medium to higher density housing. This surge in demand has occurred in both fringe and inner-city areas, in older suburbs, and near educational facilities such as universities and technical colleges. New government policy and legislation has facilitated this demand and has prompted revised structure plans with increased density zonings in the various cities where the need has occurred.

Many developers have taken advantage of these new trends and changes in the marketplace. Some have been highly successful and have specialised in a specific market niche. Unfortunately, there have also been many amateur developers who have failed. Having heard how much money is being made, they believe that this is a get-rich-quick scheme and have been short-sighted and unprofessional in their approach to their developments.

## Types of higher density housing

Several housing developments fall under this category of development, but they can be broken into two main groups, namely:

1. Grouped dwellings — this group includes properties such as townhouses, villas and retirement villages. In terms of housing form, a group dwelling usually is one of a group of two or more homes constructed at the same time, with each dwelling having its own private garden area attached.
2. Multiple dwellings — this group includes apartments and, more traditionally, flats. This building form is defined as those dwellings in a group of more than one where any part of a dwelling is built vertically above the part of any other.

## Benefits and risks

The following benefits and risks apply to higher density residential developments.

### Benefits

*Efficient use of land*

With the increase in coverage (the allowable roof cover on a building site) and plot ratios (the allowable building floor area on a building site), higher density residential areas usually utilise any developable land to its full extent. Generally, land with a higher density zoning is at a premium in terms of real estate prices. They are in prime positions, therefore forcing developers to build to the maximum allowable units on the site to capitalise on their investment.

*Variety of sizes and prices*

Experienced developers do not build and sell only one typical floor plan. They try to incorporate as many flexible designs as possible to cater to the broader taste of the market. By using a standard format, they can vary the room combinations and floor areas.

### Less sophistication required

As the units are standardised and, at times, the elevations are not seen from all sides, less elaborate detailing is required for both the internal and external parts of the buildings. Depending on the market niche, standard finishes can be used to all the units, unless the buyers request changes.

### Broader market

Depending on their location, higher density residential developments cater to a broader market. Not only do they provide for most people looking for a home with convenient facilities within proximity, but they also attract investors looking for a long-term investment in a good location and with minimal maintenance requirements.

### Better control

Unlike several single home developments where the developer is building in different locations, the higher density development, being on a single site, can be better controlled. For instance, preliminary costs (such as set-up cost) are reduced, and there is a continuity and flow of work for tradespeople, thus allowing management to control the flow of materials on site.

## Risks

### Exposure to over-building

As these developments are greater in number and therefore take longer to build, you may be midway through the project and be caught at the tail end of the boom cycle, thus leaving you with several unsold units. In the case of high-rise apartments, the building must be completed in a specified contract period, even if only 50 per cent of the units may have been sold.

### Higher demands for management

The higher amount of building activity, together with a larger number of clients to deal with, requires more staff and, therefore, more experienced management.

*Higher demands for finance*

These projects require more substantial budgets and, therefore, more personal equity into the development. To give you peace of mind and your lender, you should sell as many units off the plan before you start building. Regrettably, this is easier said than done, as buyers are becoming more astute when buying through this method.

*Shifts in consumer taste*

To attract buyers and renters, developers and their designers are continually creating new concepts, which invariably set new trends. Developers must keep in touch with these new ideas so that their own proposed development is in line with the latest consumer taste.

## Development strategy

Most of the developers in the higher density residential category, especially builders, sell the units in their development so that they can plan and start their next project. It is often the case for the builder-developer who has a large workforce and is looking for additional work to keep his or her staff employed.

On the other hand, an investor–developer would sell part of the development and retain several units for rental, which form part of a long-term investment strategy. The investor–developer, is usually a businessperson running his or her own business (other than a building company) and would use the services of several professional consultants. The profit margin would not be as high compared to builder-developer as there would be fees and charges and a builder's margin that would have to be paid out.

The strategy you choose will depend on whether you are a builder or an investor–developer.

## Market demand

The demand for higher density housing is driven by the same population growth and migration factors affecting small residential developments. Still, there are specific differences between the need for these two types of residential development.

### Change in lifestyle

Profound economic changes, improved facilities, new technology and better health mean that many people have changed their life-styles. We now find both partners in a young relationship working and more women following a career path before starting a family. It increases the demand for more compact, easy-care and convenient styles of living.

### Travelling distances

With the increase in population, new suburbs are expanding at a rapid rate in areas away from the central business district (CBD) and major leisure and recreational activities, thus making travelling times to these venues and locations longer and more expensive. Most higher density residential developments are located closer to these activities and have, therefore, become more attractive.

### Ageing population

The ageing population in Australia means that there will be a constant demand for retirement and compact unit-style living. It is the inevitable result of the number of births remaining at low levels over a long period associated with increasing life expectancy. As growth slows, the population ages progressively.

## Location analysis

In searching for the ideal location for higher density housing, the same principles apply as for smaller housing developments; however, the characteristic differences would be:

- shopping facilities should be within walking distance, especially for elderly people
- restaurants and recreation facilities should be close at hand, especially for the young, career-minded group
- public transport is a priority
- public open space (such as parks, playgrounds and reserves) should be close by
- the site should be within a certain radius of the CBD or a major business area.

# Site analysis

Again, the same principles that apply to the smaller residential developments are applied to analysing a site of a higher density. The few differences are listed below.

## Group dwellings

To reduce the expense of retaining walls, build on land that is relatively flat with a reasonable gradient for stormwater run-off and ensure that all the essential services, such as water, electricity, gas and sewerage are located near the development site.

## Multiple dwellings

The slope of the site is not such a critical factor, especially if the site has a view. Check the soil conditions as the structural loading may require expensive piling in unstable soil.

## Shape of site

In terms of economies of scale, it is always better that the plans of the units are similar, and this would require a regularly shaped site. Exercise caution with an irregularly shaped site, as you may end up needing a few different designs to accommodate the maximum number of units.

If you are uncertain about any condition or irregularities about a site, it is advisable that you consult your architect or designer before making any commitment.

# Market profile

The market profile of potential buyers or renters for higher density living comprises the following categories.

## Single adults

The single adult category includes unmarried people and students. Their preference for accommodation is for a larger living room area and master bedroom.

### Retirees

The retiree's group is made up of retired couples, single retired persons and people nearing retirement. Single-level homes with no stairs, or units with elevators, are a prerequisite.

### Young married couples

With both partners working, young married couples like a living and dining room combination.

### Empty nesters

With the children having left home, empty nesters are looking for a more carefree lifestyle. Preference is for a lock-up-and-go unit with minimal exterior maintenance.

### Investors

Investors are always on the look-out for a bargain, but they will buy into a development if the long-term capital growth prospects look good, and the area has a high rental demand.

Also, these potential buyers and renters are more sensitive to commuting distances, access to public transport, shopping, recreational and cultural amenities, and security issues.

## Market analysis

If you are planning a green-fields development or the development is larger than the norm, a market research company can play an important role. However, if your development is in an established area, you may find enough statistical data from previous sales and established trends, to assist with any market research. The following areas of research should be conducted to formulate the correct development brief.

### Demographics

A demographical study analysis the breakdown and profile of possible buyers. The study can be broken down into age, sex, marital status, income and occupation.

## Surrounding competition

A study should be conducted to establish the details of present and future competitors in the area and to evaluate if there is room for your proposed development. Also, it should be determined whether there is enough development margin with the present pricing structure amongst the current competitors.

## Consumer taste

Consumer taste will vary from area to area and research into the present and future consumer trends, and taste needs to be conducted. These trends can be analysed in terms of architectural taste, accommodation and planning.

## Consumer demand

Analysis of growth patterns in terms of population and immigration, both present and future, will have to be evaluated to justify the construction of the development.

## Present and possible future rental

Present and possible future rent is an essential element of establishing your financial gearing. Will the current and future rentals cover the development mortgage should the market fall into a recession?

## Present and possible prices of units

Determining the present and possible prices of units will assist in establishing whether a profit will be achieved after development costs have been deducted. For developments that are new in concept, it may be challenging to determine the correct market price, which ordinarily relies on past sales and several assumptions.

# Development team

Creating a competent development team is not merely a case of briefing several consultants. Experience has shown me that the team must be led and coordinated by an experienced and motivated development or project manager. If you have the in-house staff available, it is in your best interest to keep strict control of the project, but if this is not the case, you should be careful in the selection and appointment of the consultants, as they may not have the same objectives as you. Because they may not have quite the same financial incentives, consultants may not achieve the same results as the actual developer.

### Development / Project manager

Depending on the scale of the development and the experience of the developer, a development or project manager can be useful. Their role is to act on behalf of the developer or investment group, ensuring a project's viability so that it can be financed, and the projected returns are achieved.

### Town planner

If the project is a controversial one, has complex planning restrictions or if a developer wants to stretch the permissible zoning laws, a knowledgeable town planner can be handy.

### Architect

Experience is a critical factor when employing an architect to design this type of project. Good architects will know the tricks of creating tight but functional spaces, while also understanding the necessity of cost-saving design and planning.

### Quantity surveyor

The sort of services offered by a quantity surveyor will depend mainly on the size and complexity of the development. A building estimator may be used where a development is based on a sub-contracting system, and the developer does his or her own feasibility.

### Engineers

As most higher density residential developments are more significant in scale, several engineers should be appointed to fulfil specific roles. Depending on the type and scale of the project, these engineers can include geotechnical, civil, structural, mechanical, electrical, hydraulics, traffic and acoustic disciplines.

### Land surveyor

As most higher density residential developments are sold on a strata-title basis, a competent land surveyor who has a good understanding of the various regulations, especially the Strata Title Act 1967, is essential.

### Conveyancer

As the transfer and settlement of sales are paramount to your cash flow, especially in this type of development, an inexperienced and inefficient conveyancer can cost the project money.

### Lawyer

Lawyers draft purchase agreements, especially if the units in the project are to be sold off the plan. They may be also required if your planning approval has been refused and you decide to take your case to the tribunal.

## Design considerations

As mentioned earlier, the key to a successful higher density residential development is the appointment of an experienced architect who understands the needs of the consumer and has the skills to implement a cost-effective design. A good architect will also take into consideration the following elements.

### Theme

If a particular character or theme is adopted, it should follow through to all design elements of the buildings. Creating a unique theme not only establishes the development's identity but also gives the development a marketing edge.

### Scale

The scale, height and density of the development should suit the characteristics of the surrounding area. Ensure that the buildings do not appear overbearing and claustrophobic. Create an ambience with good vistas.

## Privacy

Planning for privacy can become a problem when density requirements are high. Designers should use their skills to not only plan for visual privacy but also prevent noise penetration between units or from outside.

## Natural light

The internal planning should incorporate as much natural light as possible. It can be achieved by having larger windows, which provides not only better ventilation but also a greater sense of space. Be careful, however, of having large windows facing the hot western sun.

## Energy conservation

With our extreme climatic conditions, architects and designers should plan units with the correct orientation, thereby reducing the need for air-conditioning and artificial heating.

## Security

Security in higher density developments has become an important design factor. Incorporating various security systems will enhance the sale of the units.

## Maintenance-free

Ongoing external maintenance can become a burden to a body corporate, which will often increase levies. More buyers and investors are aware of these problems and are attracted to developments with less maintenance.

## Communal facilities

Depending on the size of the development and to make the project more marketable, the developer should consider incorporating certain communal facilities such as a swimming pool, gymnasium or workshop.

## Cost factors

Compared to smaller residential developments, a higher density project will require a more detailed feasibility study and should consider the following factors.

- land purchase and settlement cost
- rezoning cost (if necessary)
- connection fees — including all essential services such as water, electricity, gas and sewerage
- bulk services (water, electricity, sewerage and stormwater) — if they are not adjacent to the property the cost of providing such services could have a major impact on the project
- site cost — is there a gentle fall across the site and are there any large trees to be removed?
- construction cost — determine the sort of contract you will use
- holding cost — if you can, plan your phases to suit your cash flow
- escalation cost — consider this when establishing the sale price of the units
- development approval and building plan fees
- development manager's fees
- project manager's fees
- professional fees
- insurance — employ a competent broker and read all the fine print
- rates and taxes
- transportation levy and any other government levies or fees
- external development cost (road widening)
- bank charges and fees
- marketing and commissions.

## Finance

The financing of multiple-residential unit developments will depend greatly on your feasibility study but, more importantly, on whether the financier has market evidence in terms of sales within the development area. This evidence is critical, as most financiers will base their lending decisions on this factor and whether there is still a demand for such a development.

In some instances, pre-sales or off-the-plan sales are critical to gain project finance — sometimes up to 100 per cent pre-sales have been required before finance has been approved. However, in most cases, financiers will require up to 50 per cent pre-sales or enough pre-sales to cover the debt they are proving for the project.

While the number of pre-sales is essential, the nature of the sales, especially regarding the type of buyer, is also significant. For example, financiers will view a higher portion of sales to the owner-occupiers, as opposed to investors, more favourably as it shows that the developer has a quality product that meets owner-occupier's demand.

## Building Contract

If you are not a builder-developer, the type of contract to be signed will be dependent on the size of the project and possibly the phasing of a group dwelling development. Your architect or development manager would be able to advise you on which contract would be applicable. Whichever contract you use, ensure that you have rates for variations confirmed before formalising the contract, as invariably your purchasers will request alterations to your standard plans or specifications.

## Marketing

Consider the following when marketing your development:
- If your development is a reasonable size and will take several months to complete, it may be preferable to have your own marketing division. Not only will you have better control over the marketing, but you will also have sales consultants dedicated to and focused on selling your project. If you follow this route, make sure that you employ experienced salespeople who understand the scheme and construction principles.
- If you must use external agents, make sure that you keep them on their toes and that they keep their promises.
- Using an off-the-plan sales system in marketing will require

some excellent presentation drawings and advertising material. Modern computer-aided-design (CAD) software can create virtual walk-throughs of various interiors so that buyers can visualise the finished product.

- Some purchasers will not buy homes or units off the plan, so a completed display unit would assist in marketing. The display unit should never be the more extensive and better unit as purchasers would expect the same, and this could lead to disappointments and possible disputes.

## Conclusion

With the influx of migration, baby boomers reaching retirement age, natural population growth and the scarcity of land close to the city, a golden opportunity has been created for residential developers. Most developers tend to sell their product to the public, but this is not the way to get rich, especially after-tax issues have been considered. Astute developers who have accumulated significant wealth have rented out their units instead, providing themselves with excellent cash flow in their retirement years.

Instead of waiting for a government pension or for your super-annuation to payout (which may eventually dry up), start building a portfolio of housing units. If you are concerned about over-gearing then sell one part of the development but retain the other portion for rental or get an equity partner involved.

# Chapter 13

# OFFICE DEVELOPMENTS

## Introduction

The present-day office is a complex and unpredictable environment. With the daily introduction of new technology, office planning is in a constant state of flux, expanding in one area, streamlining in another, replacing and redefining responsibilities and procedures. Therefore, office space developers should establish detailed sets of user requirements and evaluate and implement solutions that fulfil these needs. Research techniques should be used to ensure that the final development solutions are not arrived at by guesswork but are the results of fully informed decisions backed up by objective and systematically gathered data.

Office developments can be classified as commercial buildings and, while they are functionally different, they still have several key similarities to that of retail or industrial developments. They are generally occupied by government departments, companies, partnerships and professionals, and tend to be in or near major business district areas. However, with the advent of modern technology, this has changed. The development of the internet and social media has created a situation where more people are now working from home or co-sharing office space.

## Types of office developments

Office developments can range in size from small to large, accommodating a one-person small business to a multidisciplinary corporation and can, therefore, be broken into the following categories.

### Renovated house

In more recent times and due to zoning changes, we have seen several homes in older suburbs and along major arterial roads renovated and converted to professional offices. These conversions are generally developed by owner-occupiers such as real estate agents, doctors and dentists, or by smaller investors.

### Strata-title offices

Strata-title offices are smaller office units within an office block that is managed by a body corporate. Generally, these strata office blocks are developed on the fringes of the CBD. The units are either rented out by investors or used and owned by smaller businesses that may have been part of the original development syndicate.

### Office parks

Over the last decade, office parks have become more popular and are typically developed in decentralised suburban areas where land is less expensive. The development is made up of smaller, two- to three-storey office blocks, which are surrounded by well-landscaped gardens and open areas.

### Multistorey office blocks

A city's population density and economic wellbeing can be identified by the size and scale of its office towers. Over the years, commercial ego and identity have seen developers and large corporations attempting to build taller and more exciting office blocks, better known as skyscrapers.

Also, office developments are graded as follows:
- A grade — high-quality finishes suitable for a corporate tenant
- B grade — medium- to high-quality finishes and defined by its location
- C grade — standard finishes and located in less prominent positions.

## Benefits and risks

As with all development, there are benefits and risks. Below are some of the key benefits and risks for office developments.

### Benefits

The major benefits of office buildings over other real estate developments include the following.

*Higher potential returns*

Compared to residential developments, the returns on offices can be better if they are developed in the right location. Renting or selling is based on a rate per square metre and calculated on existing or proposed leases. Because of this, the construction or replacement cost does not hold much value when compared to the locality and rental agreements.

*Economy of scale*

If designed correctly, not much space is wasted in office developments, and the leasable area can be maximised. External finishes and structural elements are standardised, bringing the economies of scale into play.

*Relatively efficient use of land*

With inner-city office developments, developers build to the maximum allowable plot ratios to maximise their returns. Office parks and renovated home offices, which are generally located on the outskirts of the city, are more liberal in their planning.

*Anchor tenants can provide cash flow stability.*

Securing a 'blue-chip' company (a sizable, well-established business with steady and largely predictable profits) or a government department as a long-term tenant can provide a stable income to the investor developer. (With residential tenants the leases are much shorter; therefore, the returns are reduced by temporary vacancies and the cost of advertising.)

*A multi-tenant building can offer cash-flow diversification.*

More significant office developments can provide diversification in lease negotiations. To attract a major blue-chip tenant, the developer may have to reduce the asking rental; however, the return can be made up from smaller tenants who want to locate close to the blue-chip company.

*Rental escalation provides additional inflation protection.*

With all leases in office developments, there is a built-in annual rental escalation. This escalation can be linked to either the consumer price index or a negotiated percentage. It means the rental return does not fall or lag behind regular inflationary figures.

## Risks

While office developments show higher returns and are more sophisticated than residential developments, the following risks apply.

*Larger financial capital required.*

The building and land costs require more capital investment compared to residential developments. The price of land is generally higher for an office development unless a well-located piece of land is bought as residential and later rezoned to commercial. Building costs can be higher, especially if lifts and the number of storeys increase.

*The supply and demand for office space are highly cyclical.*

Office vacancy statistics brought out by the Australian Bureau of Statistics are used by the real estate industry as a guide as they help to forecast the supply and demand for office space. After a building boom, there is generally a surplus of office space, and rentals are very favourable. It is followed by higher demand and premium rental rates just before the peak of the cycle.

*Tenants are more sophisticated in negotiations.*

Most tenants seeking office space are businesspeople and, therefore, take a business approach when negotiating a lease. The developer and his or her agent or real estate broker will require robust negotiation techniques.

*Alterations to suit tenant requirements.*

To secure a tenant, a developer may be required to make several alterations, which may not be suitable for other future tenants. If you must undertake these alterations, ensure that the tenant signs a long-term lease so that you can secure a return on the additional investment cost.

*Higher management cost*

More significant office buildings will require efficient management and accounting facilities. Depending on the size of the development, a full-time property manager may be necessary to ensure the smooth operation of the building.

## Development strategy

The strategy applied to speculative office development will depend on the target market and whether the developer's interest is based on quick profit or a long-term investment.

If the approach is to achieve an immediate return, the developer will have to build, lease and sell to an institutional investor. Some institutional investors prefer office developments as an investment compared to retail or other forms of real estate. The reason for this is that management and investment security is better and safer. The design of office developments is more straightforward and less varied compared to retail developments where tenants have essential and diverse requirements.

Whichever approach or strategy the developer takes, he or she may end up developing the following.

## Custom-built offices

These offices may be built for government or large institutional corporations, which are broken into several departments ranging from two people to several hundred. These departments may have to be connected through central cores or service links. In developing a custom-built project, the developer should seek a long-term lease — the minimum being ten years. Care should also be taken not to risk building deep, airconditioned space, which will reduce the possibility of subletting should the tenant fail or when the lease is terminated.

## Multi-tenancy offices

When a developer decides to develop and lease office space in small parcels, the need for deep offices and single access is less pronounced. The appropriate building is subdivided into a variety of different sized areas with each having its own access. While this approach may have less risk, it will require more management.

# Market demand

The demand for new office space is generally determined by whether there are new business start-ups and expansion of operations by existing tenants. However, this demand is very cyclical and is prone to the effects of supply and demand. Compared to residential space, office space generally tends to be more reactive to these fluctuations. In a market where there is an undersupply of office space, there is a reduction in the vacancy rates. In contrast, in an oversupplied market, the vacancy rate is higher, and prospects for steady rental growth are a lot fewer. It can be seen from the table below.

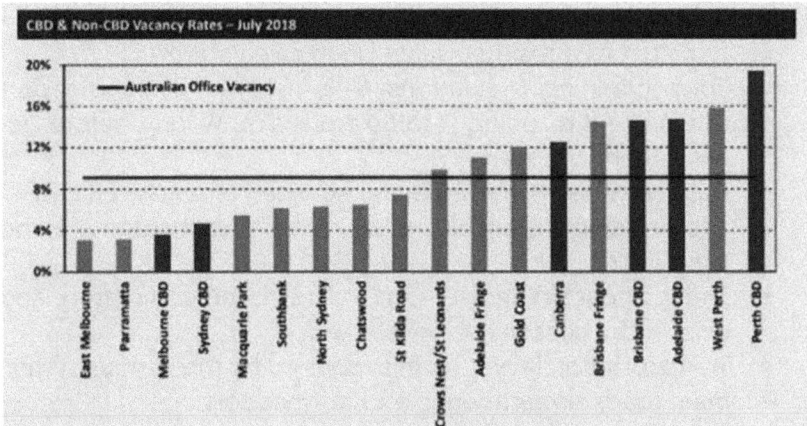

Table 13.1: Australian CBD office vacancy — percentage comparative analysis

In addition to the economic cycle, either the movement of businesses from other areas or the expansion of a multinational company seeking a presence in new regions can generate the demand.

## Location analysis

The location for developing new office space will be mostly dependent on research findings. This research might establish that there is a trend away from high rise CBD office blocks and towards office parks closer to suburban areas. The following factors will have to be considered when purchasing a development site:

- access to public transport
- exposure to major arterial roads and public transport facilities
- adjacent complementary businesses
- ease of public access
- access to restaurants and conference facilities
- advertising exposure.

## Site analysis

Site analysis is intended to elicit all information about the site, demonstrating the advantages and restrictions so that the development team can make all decisions concerning existing conditions. The team should look at the following:

- Land cost — is the asking price related to market conditions or has a residual value been calculated?
- Town planning regulations — is a town planning report available? If rezoning is to take place, how long before development can start?
- Bulk services — are essential services of water, electricity and sewerage available? If not, at what cost could they be supplied?
- Traffic impact analysis — has a study been completed, and what is the cost to the developer?
- Transportation levy — is this required by the various states' main roads departments, and at what cost?
- Access — are both vehicular and pedestrian access convenient and well located?
- Neighbours — how do the surrounding buildings affect the development? Are these compatible?

## Market profile

The market seeking new office space can be broken into various categories, namely:
- single operators
- small businesses
- medium businesses
- large corporations
- small government departments
- larger government offices.

While one would expect the office tenant to be price sensitive in terms of where to rent, there are other factors that the typical tenant seeks in office development, namely:
- prestige location
- special amenities
- special services.

## Market analysis

Before a design brief or any significant financial commitment is made on an office development, a market analysis covering the following factors should be investigated. In analysing the demand for new space, the developer must predict the employment figures in industries using office space and the amount of area that will be required. Measuring these factors involves researching the following.

### The increase in national employment

It involves researching and watching the movement of:
- national economic variables such as the gross national product
- the local economic variables, such as the influx of new industries and the expansion of existing industries.

### The shifts in employment structures

It involves keeping a close watch on:
- the changes in the service-orientated industries
- the increase and decrease in the employment of government civil servants.

### The changing trends in office space use

It involves analysing current and future trends:

- the decrease in spatial needs and more efficient use of office space due to new office machinery such as computers and photocopying machines
- the effect of modern communication technology, such as mobile phones and the internet, which decreases the necessity for travel.

## Development team

An essential ingredient in accomplishing a successful office development is an interdisciplinary team of consultants who will ensure that the planning does not overlook or exclude any element of office user and that the solutions developed for the project are integrated. The make-up of the development team depends on the size of the development, the time allocated for the project and the scope of the development. There is no set formula for team membership. The membership should be flexible and should be tailored to the development at hand.

## Design considerations

As pointed out earlier, types of office users vary from a single business operator to a large corporation and, therefore, there is no set planning formula to accommodate the diverse users unless there is a client with specific needs. Also, certain site constraints may force the architect to design a building maximising the site potential. A typical case would be the design of a city office block where the form and aesthetics are considered a priority and the need for occupants secondary. However, there are two underlying principles which are critical in office design: flexibility and environmental requirements.

### Flexibility

The development team has the option of adopting a concept of open plan or closed offices, or a combination of the two. All workplaces should be easily rearranged to accommodate the formation of new groups and the addition or relocation of new users. The final layout type will be dependent upon the user and organisational needs.

**Environmental requirements**

The establishment of environmental requirements is a crucial planning step because it will address what must be achieved to make the internal space a design success. These requirements are not design guidelines but design necessities, and are as follows:

- The technical acoustic systems must be flexible to accommodate new layouts and different densities.
- Lighting levels in all workplaces must be to acceptable standards to handle conventional reading and writing tasks.
- Lighting throughout the interior must be flexible to accommodate the rearrangement and addition of users.
- The fire and safety requirements must be able to accommodate different users and planning layouts.
- Power, telephone, computer networking and other electronic wiring should be flexible and able to be rearranged to accommodate different densities and users.
- Air-conditioning and ventilation should be able to accommodate users in different locations.

# Cost factors

In addition to the land and typical development costs, the following design factors can affect the overall cost and feasibility of an office development.

**Floor space economics**

The plot ratio exercise is well understood by developers who specialise in office buildings. The developer will instruct an architect to design the building using the maximum allowable building area and extract the maximum leasable area. When buying land for office development, developers do not base the cost of land on the ground-floor space; instead, they assess its actual value relative to the allowable plot ratio.

### The ratio of net leasable area to the gross floor area

The relationship between the gross and net leasable area is critical in an office plan. The closer the two figures, the more profitable the development will be. The ratio between net and gross varies from building to building and is not only influenced by the skill of the architect but also by the physical requirements of the site and planning authorities.

### The ratio of the external wall to the floor area

One of the more expensive elements in any building is the external perimeter wall. The wider the gap between the external walls to the floor area, the more savings made on the building cost. For example, a square or rectangular building plan has less perimeter walling than an H-shaped plan of a similar floor area. However, in trying to achieve a better ratio, the designer should be careful not to increase the cost of artificial lighting.

### The artificial or natural environment and services required.

The initial capital cost of artificial lighting and mechanical ventilation could be relatively expensive, not only in the short term but also during the life of the building. Besides the ongoing maintenance, there is also the problem of energy waste since artificial services cater mainly for multi-use, rather than individual use. Designing offices where these costs can be reduced, and as much natural lighting and ventilation as possible are incorporated into the new building will benefit the developer and the environment.

### The type of structure

The structure of an office building can play an essential role in the overall economics and planning of a project. It can be seen in cases where underground parking is required and where the land cost is high and space at a premium, the structural elements are generally designed around economical parking and vehicular circulation.

### The amount of parking

Where to position the car parking facilities is a big part of office design and the economics of the development. Its primary effect is that it restricts floor space and the structural grid pattern. As the provision of parking adds significantly to the overall building cost, developers charge a rental based on a rate per bay.

## Marketing

The marketing of offices will depend upon the location, the type of offices and the type of users being targeted. In most major cities, extensive finance, law and accounting firms, and major corporations tend to concentrate in the CBD where they can interact with each other. It also applies to government departments, the stock exchange, law courts and the taxation office. On the fringe of the CBD, there is a tendency for smaller companies and professional practices to congregate. These smaller businesses do not necessarily need daily contact with other companies in the CBD.

Besides the location of the development, other important factors that should be highlighted in the marketing brochure and other marketing material are:

- its accessibility
- the general external appearance of the building
- the quality of the entrance lobbies
- the quality of and allowance for carpets and partitions
- availability of parking and neighbouring facilities.

These factors will all influence the tenant's decision as they will view them from their specific business requirements and, more importantly, to attract customers.

## Viability

As soon as the developer has established an estimate of future revenues based on a study of the demand for office building space, he or she will undertake a feasibility study by applying cash-flow and residual value techniques like those discussed in previous chapters.

While conducting this study, the developer will have to consider expenses that are particular to office buildings. These can include items such as:

- cleaning services
- security attendants
- parking attendants
- on-site engineers to handle facilities and equipment maintenance.

## Types of tenants

One of the critical elements to successful office development and investment is securing good stable tenants. With office developments, various types of tenants will make up the tenant mix in a building. They include:

### Blue Chip Tenants

Blue-chip tenants include government departments, banking institutions and large multi-national corporations such as insurance groups. Most of these tenants generally sign a long-term lease of at least ten years with an option to renew. Securing a blue-chip tenant is virtually a guarantee of steady income, which will be attractive to any investor if the developer decides to sell.

### Medium size business tenants

Medium size business tenants are generally made up professional services companies such as law firms, accountants, publicly listed companies, and so on. These tenants tend to a minimum of 5 years with options to renew for a similar period. Securing these tenants are appealing to investors as historically, they have proven to be reliable and secure tenants.

### Small business tenants

Small business tenants make up most of the tenancies. They generally take the minimum term lease but on average most would take out a 3-year term lease. Historically, there is a high business failure rate with most small businesses. Therefore, it would be necessary to check the profile of the company and especially how long they have been in business. With new businesses, it would be worthwhile to do a credit check through a credit bureau, and if necessary, a credit check on the directors or owners.

## Office Leases

Office leases are generally drafted in a standard format, and many established landlords and commercial real estate brokers have their pre-printed documents with certain conditions added as negotiated. With larger corporate tenants, it is not unusual for firm negotiations to take place and for the developer to make certain concessions and have a new lease drafted.

The more essential terms and conditions negotiated by the developer and tenant are:

- Term — the term of the lease should be a minimum of three years, and preferably more if possible.
- Rental — try to obtain a commercially prevalent and market-acceptable rental and a due date for payment. Apply penalties for any late payments.
- Rental escalation — this could either be a fixed percentage or in line with the CPI.
- Use of premises — restrictions or building regulations, and the types of business that are allowed in the building should be defined.
- Outgoings — generally in commercial leases the tenant is responsible for the outgoings. Outgoings include rates and taxes, water and electricity.
- Tenant work — any alterations to be completed by the developer/landlord on behalf of the tenant should be defined.
- Tenant's work — the landlord, should approve any alterations performed by the tenant during the lease and the building should be restored to its original state at the end of the lease.
- Option — this means including in the lease an option to extend the term of the lease or an option for additional space.
- Rebuilding — the lease should contain a clause allowing the landlord to rebuild and renovate.
- Destruction — this clause should be inserted to protect both parties in case of destructive events such as fires or floods.

## Conclusion

Residential development is not everybody's cup of tea. You have to deal with buyers and tenant's unreasonable demands and emotional outbursts when the home is not completed as anticipated which will not suit an impatient developer. So, if you are looking for a development and investment in a commercial area and do not want to get involved in a project that is capital intensive, a small office development is an ideal way to start.

However, if you find a more substantial office development, you do not necessarily have to go it alone — arrange a syndicate with a few friends or business associates. This concept worked very successfully in my first office development, which consisted of a syndicate of six investors. We developed eight strata office units. After the completion of the project, the six investors received their unit at cost. The two other two units were sold at market value, and the profit made was distributed equally amongst the six of us, reducing the total capital commitment and increased our nett equity.

# Chapter 14

# *RETAIL DEVELOPMENTS*

## Introduction

All communities require retail outlets and shopping centres to be built, just as they require housing and education facilities. The development of and investment in commercial retail outlets has many more requirements and risks than other development projects; however, they can produce higher income and growth prospects if analysed correctly and cautiously.

## Types of retail developments

Commercial retail includes developments such as:

- Convenience store — this is the traditional corner convenience store typically found in older suburban areas or at petrol stations.
- Strip shopping — this can be described as a continuous line of shops such as showrooms usually found along major arterial routes.
- Neighbourhood shopping centre (1,000m2 to 5,000m2) — the neighbourhood shopping centre has one major anchor tenant such as a supermarket together with several smaller speciality shops.
- District shopping centre (5,000m² to 20,000m²) — the district shopping centre has at least two anchor tenants, one of which is generally is a department store, and may also include banks and professional offices together with speciality shops.

- Regional shopping centre (20,000m² plus) — developed with at least two or more major tenants such as supermarkets and department stores, and other smaller speciality stores selling general merchandise and apparel.
- Discount Warehouse centres – a typical complex consists of several warehouses grouped together offering retail goods at factory prices.
- Mixed-use retail centres - retail outlets are now becoming part of a higher mix integrated with other classes of buildings, especially with entertainment and restaurants.
- Transit retail centres - successful retail buildings are all about foot traffic and with the volume of pedestrian traffic coming from buses and trains, it makes sense to create a retail component as part of the mix.

Relatively inexperienced individuals or small syndicates can develop corner convenience stores, strip shopping and neighbourhood shopping centres. In contrast, the development of the larger centres is usually undertaken by experienced, knowledgeable and financially able development groups. These larger centres involve complex research analysis, smart planning, correct financial structures, various leasing options and expert management. While each of these categories has its characteristics, there are similar basic principles that apply to each when developing and financing.

## Benefits and risks

While there are significant financial benefits with retail developments, it comes with substantial risks. Below is a comparison between the two.

### Benefits

Developing a retail outlet can be exciting and rewarding, and the main benefits are listed as follows.

*Greater capital growth*
As with most commercial property, the value of the buildings increases according to the escalation in rent. Also, due to these

developments having longer leases, the potential long-term growth in commercial properties is generally higher than in residential properties.

## Cash-flow potential
Tenants generally pay the major portion of the operational and promotional cost, together with outgoings.

## Care by tenants
As retail tenants must survive in business, they tend to create ways to maintain or grow the standards of their business and will generally take care of the property.

## Ease of financing
If the right location is found, key tenants are signed on long-term leases, and a viable return is evaluated, then finance is generally, easily procured.

## Monopoly opportunities
This situation is created if there is no other land within the neighbourhood available for another competing retail centre.

## Risks

Like all the other developments, retail centres involve several risks. They also have unique problems, such as:

## Inefficient use of land
Because of parking requirements in retail centres, a great portion of development land cannot be used for building unless basement parking is provided which is expensive to build and maintain.

## High land cost
Many factors contribute to the high land cost, including the shortage of developable land within an established neighbourhood and the inefficient use of land due to parking requirements.

## The scale of development finance
A large-scale building with high quality finishes to attract

consumers to the centre requires a more significant financial capital commitment.

### Tenant business failure

Statistics reveal that a considerable proportion of new businesses tend to fail in their early years and modern shopping centres seem to attract these types of tenants.

### Risk of new centres opening

New retail centres create new competition a specific area and could attract your consumers and key tenants by offering favourable leases.

### High level of management required

Tenant requests, high levels of maintenance, security and promotions require specialist, full-time management.

### Higher exposure to tenant problems

Business problems, rent increases and tenant competition within the same centre creates an environment for tenant complaints.

### Risk of obsolescence

To attract consumers, retail buildings must continuously keep up with new architectural trends and finishes, especially in high traffic areas of the building.


## Development strategy

A retail real estate developer may be a private individual or company, or an institutional investor or developer such as an insurance company. These developers provide all the necessary expertise and finance and take all the essential risk. Larger institutions are in a better position than most to develop largescale shopping centres as their strategy is based on long-term investment, and any financial loss is generally recouped over a period of years.

Private developers should be more cautious with this retail developments as their financial gearing position makes them more vulnerable to any mistakes, no matter how small. If the private developer is not holding the building as a long-term investment but intends to develop and sell to a major investment institution, he or she can make a considerable profit by managing the development professionally. These investment institutions are prepared to pay a premium if the centre is well-located, and if the developer takes the risk (rather than themselves). To lessen the risk, the private developer should try to sell the development before the start of construction.

## Market demand

Shopping is a social requirement, and the same forces that create a need for housing and education facilities will be significant in analysing the demand for new shopping and retail outlets. While online shopping is growing, it will not eliminate the need for consumers to leave our homes as human beings are by nature, social creatures.

Research by the Australian Bureau of Statistics indicate that retail turnover accounts for a major share (about 40 per cent) of expenditure-based estimates of gross domestic product. It is also an essential economic indicator and a guide to consumer confidence. The main elements that will fuel the demand for additional retail space are:
- population growth
- migration
- spending power and consumer confidence.

## Location analysis

Determining an ideal location for a specific retail centre and measuring whether the trading area will support such a development requires consideration of the following:
- travelling distances and travelling time
- consumer perception of travel distance and time
- highway patterns
- visibility
- relationship to other centres
- future expansion
- the vacancy rate in neighbouring centres

- consumer retail expenditure patterns
- tenant mix relative to the community's socioeconomic character

## Site analysis

As the capital investment in retail developments is relatively high, several variables related to the land and the proposed buildings should be carefully considered. These include the following.

### Zoning

Establish whether the site is already zoned for retail commercial purposes. If not, determine how long the rezoning will take and the associated cost.

### Site characteristics

Characteristics of the site include the soil conditions, falls (or slopes) across the site, existing vegetation and trees and stormwater run-off. You will need to establish whether the design can be incorporated into the existing conditions.

### Bulk services

Determine whether essential services such as water, sewerage, roads, telephone, gas and electricity are available. If not, what is the cost of installation to the developer?

### Access and egress

Work out if one can access the site from a major arterial road. Does the present access and egress to the site comply with good traffic design, and is it convenient to the customer? If not, is it required of the developer to do a traffic impact analysis and to redesign and reconstruct a new road layout?

### Restrictions on site

Determine if there are any easements, covenants, zoning restrictions or land rights on the site, and whether these can be removed if they impose upon the design.

### Authorities

Establish whether there are any other authorities besides the regular local council who have jurisdiction over the site.

### Transport

Look into public transport in the area. Is the site well located to a train station or main public bus route?

### Adjacent neighbours

Examine the zoning and existing land use and buildings. Will the new centre impose upon the lifestyle and comfort of the existing neighbours?

## Market analysis

In assessing the potential of a retail development, several considerations need to be weighed up. The market analysis should be carried out by experienced professionals and should include:

- the identification of the catchment area (that is, the number of consumers within a particular area who will use the shopping centre facilities)
- analysis of household expenditure within the catchment area
- analysis of future population trends and income projections within the catchment area
- a traffic survey to determine the length of the journey to the centre by car or public transport from surrounding suburbs
- a study of the types of primary and speciality stores most needed in the area
- analysis of the effect of the proposed centre on existing trading patterns in the area
- the proximity and impact of competing shops within the catchment area
- analysis of the potential sales/volume in a 10-year period
- analysis of comparative rentals within the catchment area
- assessment of retail floor area requirements in the proposed development.

The analysis of these elements indicates whether there is a need for the proposed shopping centre. In many cases, a new site may have potential, but with this information, it can be accurately gauged whether the centre should be built at a later stage or built in phases.

## Development team

Retail development like a shopping centre is complicated, and the number of interested individuals and groups so great, therefore considerable skill and determination is necessary to keep a balance between subjective desires and practical planning.

The development team must consist of several professionals with practical management skills. They must take responsibility for their decisions and give useful direction to the project. No single team member should dominate the others. It is mainly applied in a situation where the architect has strong ideas on the design, which may not be appreciated by shoppers and tenants. The team should be particularly sensitive to local attitudes, tastes and shopping habits.

The developer will only make a profit if the development is successful. In contrast, the consultants do not carry the same risk — even some prominent architects have been known to design white elephants ('pretty' buildings designed without any consideration of cost), therefore making the project unviable.

## Design principles

The planning and design of a retail development require certain critical design principles, and developers should ensure that these values are maintained and not be influenced to the contrary by architects or other consultants who may have their own beliefs. Figure 14.1 illustrates the required principles.

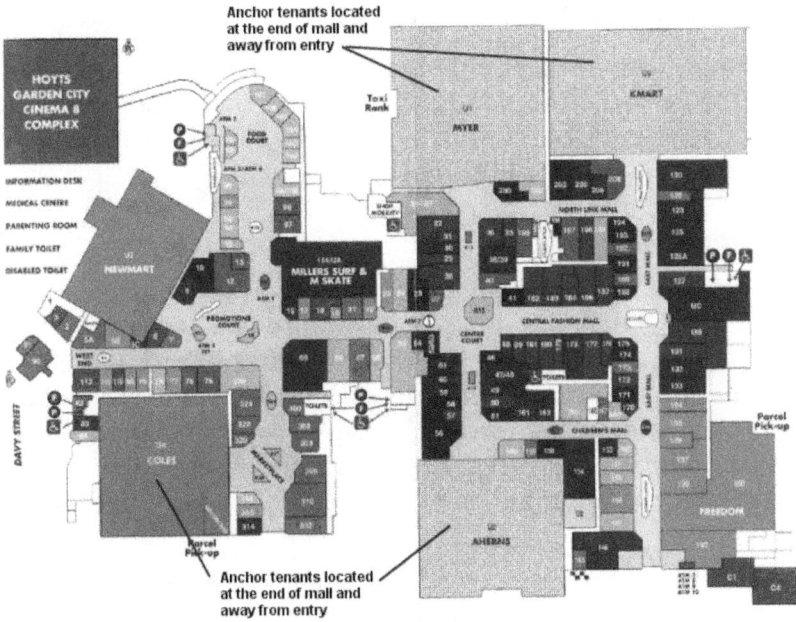

Figure 14.1: Garden City Shopping Centre
Source: Garden City Shopping Centre floor plan included with the permission of AMP Capital and Garden City Shopping Centre.

## Pedestrian flow pattern

The key to a successful shopping centre layout is unquestionably a determined pedestrian flow. The importance of this cannot be stressed enough. The ideal plan will encourage high pedestrian flow through all parts of the centre. It will not only obtain the maximum rental potential but will create a busy and lively atmosphere that all successful centres have.

## Simple layout

Keep the planning simple so that pedestrians know where they are going and where they can find individual shops. It must also be appreciated how tiring shopping can be, and resting points should be provided along the major routes. Research has shown that shoppers are prepared to walk a maximum of 250 metres from one location to another; otherwise, they lose interest.

### Good tenant mix

It is the principle whereby tenants of similar trades are grouped as it further increases pedestrian traffic. Competition amongst tenants is welcomed in a centre but be careful of excessive competition as this defeats its purpose.

### Shopfronts

Shopfronts of individual tenants should be given a certain amount of freedom to display their merchandise and their corporate identity. Shoppers' interest will wane if no merchandise is shown and adjacent tenants will suffer. Bland shopfronts such as those of banks and supermarkets should be kept away from the main body of the pedestrian route. These tenants are 'destination' shops and are typically placed at the end of the journey.

### Entrances

Care should be taken when choosing the position and design of the entrances to the centre. They should be easily identified from the exterior and have enough cover for protection against wet weather and should not be in line with prevailing winds.

### Size of centre

Research has found that the floor space limits can be based on per capita figures and should be assessed in conjunction with existing retail outlets within the catchment area. The following measurements should apply for each tenant in the type of centre specified:
- 0.35 square metres for local and other centres
- 0.28 square metres for neighbourhood centres
- 0.34 square metres for district centres
- 0.31 square metres for regional centres.

Building a centre with specifications which exceed the above guide may put a developer in a position where he or she is left with space that cannot be leased.

### Delivery and service

The planning and location of the delivery and service areas should be carefully considered. Providing a service at the rear of each store can prove to be expensive in land cost and would look unsightly from all areas. Although all major stores must have specially allocated off-loading areas, other shops can share communal spaces, hoists and corridors to receive their goods deliveries.

## Shop areas

To create a commercially successful centre, it is desirable to achieve maximum trading representation, which, therefore, makes shop frontage a premium. Shops that are laid out in an unimaginative and stereotypical structural grid often results in a situation where several shops have a similar area, depth and frontage. It must be remembered that different traders have different space needs and that higher rentals can be achieved if there is an allowance for flexibility to accommodate different frontage widths.

## Future expansion

A thriving shopping centre will probably lead to the need for future expansion, so wherever possible, some provision in the design should be made for this.

## Parking

Inadequate and inconvenient parking can frustrate a shopper before he or she even enters the main building and could create such a negative impact that the shopper does not return to the centre. Parking should be free or relatively cheap, convenient and adequate and should be planned in such a way as to minimise the walking distances to the main entrances.

# Cost factors

Aside from the regular land and building costs, retail shopping developments attract costs that are not generally associated with other types of development. These factors are listed below.

## Developer's cost

Shopping centres attract large volumes of pedestrians and motor traffic, which invariably changes the local traffic and road patterns. The developer must undertake a traffic impact analysis, which may recommend alterations to the existing road system. These costs are generally borne by the developer unless negotiated with the local authorities. Also, there may be additional costs such as the bulk supply of other essential services such as water, electricity and gas. In larger shopping centres which are not strata titled, these services are billed directly to the landlord who, in turn, meters each tenant's consumption and charges them accordingly.

## Parking requirements

Parking and traffic circulation are one of the high costs in a shopping development because of the stringent parking requirements set out by the local authorities. Where land is at a premium, the provision of such facilities can become extremely expensive, mainly where a multi-level parking area must be provided.

## Artificial environment

Shopping comfort is a prerequisite in any shopping centre design. With Australia's sweltering summers, developers should factor in the installation cost of air-conditioning and ducting.

## Enclosed mall

With enclosed malls, the requirement for artificial ventilation becomes a critical factor. However, to create the right 'shopping experience', developers have to spend a large amount of money on the quality and effect of the mall by providing quality finishes, good lighting, seating, planting and promotion areas.

## Shopfronts

To create the right street appeal in both enclosed and open malls, the developer should instruct his architect to design attractive and eye-catching shopfronts and entrances. Shopfronts with large window areas can prove to be expensive, so some developers provide a standard shopfront for a provisional sum and charge the shop owner for any additional cost incurred as a result of the tenant's requirements.

### Fire-fighting equipment

As shopping centres are public buildings with large volumes of people using them at any one time, the provision of fire-fighting equipment becomes an expensive necessity for the developer. It can include sprinkler systems, fire hydrants and fire barriers.

## Construction

Management during the construction of a retail project is a critical factor. In most retail building contracts; the construction program is always restricted to a very tight schedule. Some of the driving forces of speedy construction are the high cost of finance, the timing to meet tenants' lease conditions and, invariably, the centre needing to be opened before a major holiday period such as Christmas or Easter.

These tough conditions can lead to several mistakes if an inexperienced builder or project manager is appointed. The experienced project manager will be able to manage and co-ordinate the professional team by ensuring that documents are always submitted to the builder on time and that the builder has a minimal reason for delay. Another important aspect is the co-ordination of tenants' requirements and their various dates of occupation, as any delays can cause tensions between the developer and tenant.

## Marketing

The marketing of a shopping development starts almost at the time an offer or option to purchase a site is concluded. Acquisition of key tenants and the marketing of the development begin quietly with informal contacts known to the developer (or the developer's agent), and these can include major national retail groups and credible local companies. The attraction of high-profile key companies at the outset is helpful to the success of the development. Marketing material used at this stage need not be sophisticated, but it should illustrate the location of the proposed development and the overall project concept.

As the development progresses, the process would be to implement a full marketing program, including the appointment of the following:

- advertising agencies
- public relations officers
- leasing agents
- brochure and billboard designers.

A well-presented brochure will assist the leasing agents but, more importantly, the broker should be provided with technical data. It should consist of statistical data and descriptive material of interest to the prospective tenant and should include information such as the population of the catchment area and shopper profile. The catchment area may be broken into primary, secondary and peripheral zones. The value of these zones can vary significantly between centres located in well-established areas and those to be constructed in new suburbs that are not fully developed. The shopper profile would be categorised into income levels and purchasing power.

## Tenants

As soon as the size and type of centre has been established and a general appreciation of the accommodation has been recognised, it is essential to approach and select the key tenants, such as department stores, variety stores, specialist stores and supermarkets, for the main spaces provided. A well-designed centre with poor tenants will be a commercial disaster, whereas a poorly designed building with excellent tenants can still be a commercial success. Look for tenants who are:

- in a stable or growth industry and avoid ones with limited lifespan — credit checks with a credit bureau will assist subject to the approval and consent of the tenants
- established businesses, particularly national or known companies.

## Lease agreements

In negotiating leases with prospective tenants, the developer will find that the final lease conditions will differ significantly between the larger key anchor tenants and the smaller speciality shop lessees. The larger key tenants gain more concessions as they know that the developer requires their store in the building to obtain finance and act as a draw to the smaller satellite shops.

The following elements should be considered:

- term — leases should be for a longer-term if possible
- rent — obtain a commercially and market-acceptable rent
- rent escalation — try for the maximum but should be at least market acceptable
- rebuilding — leases should have a rebuilding and renovation clause
- destruction — a clause should be inserted to protect the developer against fires and natural disasters

## Property management

Perhaps in no other building type does management play such a critical role. The management of a shopping centre is a specialised area, and some of its methods are entirely divorced from the traditional management concepts applied to the operation of other commercial and apartment buildings. Traditional management concepts deal with the operational and maintenance aspects of the building. Property management in a shopping centre, on the other hand, must focus on public relations, leasing and promotions. It is, therefore, imperative to employ property managers with experience and a successful track record.

## Conclusion

Developing a retail outlet and especially a shopping centre can be fun, creative and very stimulating but it is not for the faint-hearted. With strict deadlines to meet, unrealistic demands by tenants and huge capital commitments, a great deal of devotion to and expertise in this type of project are necessary.

In 1990 I developed my first major shopping centre, a neighbourhood centre comprising 4,500 square metres. I made the fatal mistake of tackling the design, administration, project management, property management and construction with only a handful of staff. The development took a great deal of my time — to the point that some of my housing projects started to slip. Had I put the project out to tender and employed a more substantial building company with the resources to undertake the construction, I would have been able to manage my other projects a lot more successfully.

Before tackling a shopping centre development, ensure that you have the necessary management skills, financial resources and expert consultants, and an excellent understanding of development procedures and the functions of the various people involved.

# Chapter 15

# INDUSTRIAL DEVELOPMENTS

## Introduction

At the turn of the nineteenth century, there was a period called the industrial revolution, which saw the rapid development of machinery and large industrial buildings. Many years later, these older-style buildings are still found in heavily urbanised areas. These areas have a large concentration of freestanding factories, warehouses and supply yards, intermixed with commercial and service establishments (such as administrative offices, government buildings and financial institutions). These areas, which vary in scale according to the size of the local communities, were usually developed in the pre-highway era and located adjacent to railway lines. Physical and structural obsolescence are constant problems in these areas, as crowded streets and insufficient areas for parking and loading tend to hamper operations.

With time and new town-planning concepts, industrial development areas have moved in another direction. The modern industrial park is a concept which has evolved over the last 80 years and comprises a combination of industrial plants, warehouses, research and development laboratories and office buildings, with wide roads and decent infrastructure. During this period, private developers, transport companies and public corporations have shown that a carefully located, well-designed and adequately developed tract of land can achieve successful results for all concerned. It has been accomplished by efficient land management, by assisting the community with new employment opportunities and by providing a marketable product required by small to large industrial companies.

## Types of industrial buildings

The industrial real estate consists mainly of factories and warehouses of varying sizes and can be broken down into the following categories:

1. **Warehouses and Distribution Centres**
   These buildings range from 3,000 to thousands of sqm in one single-storey structure. They have an 18m floor to ceiling height, loading docks, truck doors, and ample parking lots to accommodate semi-trailers. They may have a small amount of office space and may be served by rail cars.

2. **Manufacturing Buildings (heavy industrial buildings)**
   These facilities house specialised equipment used to manufacture materials or products. They typically have 3-phase electric power and may also include large ductwork, pressurised air or water lines, high capacity ventilation and exhaust systems, floor drains, storage tanks and cranes.

3. **Cold Storage Buildings**
   These are specific industrial properties that are equipped to hold a large capacity of cold storage plus freezer space. They can be a standalone building or part of a distribution centre for food products.

4. **Strata factory units**
   This type falls under light industrial and is capable of housing a wide range of uses. Typically, they can include office space, research and development, showroom retail sales, light manufacturing research and development, and even small warehouse and distribution uses. They typically feature lower ceilings (under 5.5 metres) and a higher amount of office space than other industrial property types.

The type of industrial buildings found in a master planned estate are initiated and supported by local or state government to encourage and stimulate their local economy. These estates are described as:

- **Industrial Parks**
  These parks fall within a city's urban structure zoned for industrial use. They may contain oil refineries, warehouses, distribution centres and factories within or near a harbour or airport. These estates can combine a mix of production, transportation and storage facilities in the same area. Some parks have tax incentives for businesses to locate there.

- **Eco-Industrial Parks**
  An eco-industrial park (EIP) is where businesses cooperate with each other and with the local community to reduce waste and pollution, efficiently share resources and help achieve sustainable development, with the intention of increasing economic gains and improving environmental quality.

## Benefits and risks

Below is an analysis of the benefits and risks of developing industrial buildings.

### Benefits

From the investment point of view, developing industrial buildings can be rewarding for the following reasons.

*Less management required*

As there are fewer tenants (at times, only a single tenant) who occupy industrial buildings, the management of industrial real estate is less intense than other forms of development.

*Potential monopoly*

Industrial real estate is generally planned and zoned within a specific limited area. It usually creates a monopoly in pricing if there is no land left for further industrial development.

*A stable form of revenue*

If the development is designed, built and rented to suit a prime tenant, it is done mainly on the basis that a long-term lease is contracted and will bring a stable form of income to the investor for a reasonable period.

### Reduced sensitivity to neighbourhood problems

Industrial land is typically zoned early and as part of an overall urban structure plan. The town planners who establish these zones usually take into consideration that there should be no problems with future adjacent neighbours.

### Fewer landlord and tenant problems

Most industrial businesses, on average, take great care in their business, and there are generally fewer problems with these tenants compared to other forms of real estate.

## Risks

The risks in developing and investing in industrial buildings are as follows.

### Substantial capital investment required.

Although they cost less per square metre to construct than other buildings, industrial properties are much larger in floor area and have long roof-spans, so they require more capital investment.

### Less escalation potential

As most leases are long-term, the escalation clauses are at times fixed and not in line with the CPI, and therefore do not allow adjustment of escalation if inflation increases significantly.

### Changes in technology

With manufacturing and assembly technology changing at a rapid pace to increase production, industrial buildings are exposed to the risk of becoming obsolete.

### Greater exposure to government regulations

Due to the number of occupants in industrial buildings (mainly if they are being used as processing plants), the construction of these developments may have to comply with several stringent government regulations and inspections.

*More sophisticated tenants*

Tenants who occupy these buildings are generally established businesses and thus have plenty of experience negotiating leases.

*Custom-building problems*

In some cases, a developer must build the property according to a tenant's specific requirements only to find that it does not suit the general market when the term of the lease has expired.

## Development strategy

Like other developments, the strategy for an industrial project should be worked out to maximise the market potential while minimising development costs. It applies whether the developer intends to sell or hold on to the completed project as a long-term investment. Many developers would fall into the latter category, especially if they have signed a long-term lease with a credible corporate tenant.

In the case where a developer's planned project is a set of smaller industrial units aimed at the small business community, he or she may sell these units to owner-operators and investors. Alternatively, the developer may sell a percentage of the units to better his or her equity and gearing position and retain the balance as a long-term investment.

## Market demand

The demand for industrial buildings depends mainly on the employment trends in the specific industries that are most likely to use such buildings. It will also be influenced by the particular space needs of the employees in those industries.

### Employment trends

Business success depends on several variable factors, such as the national and local economies and demographics. But these factors do not necessarily affect employment in the industrial sector to the same extent. For example, employment in the shipping and cargo industry is not as sensitive to demographic changes as employment in the manufacturing retail sector. Therefore, accurate analysis of the employment in a specific industry within a particular area will determine the demand for industrial space.

### Specific space needs

Specific spatial requirements vary from industry to industry. For example, the area by square metre per employee required in the clothing industry is less than the requirements in manufacturing industries (for example, building products). It is because clothing manufacturing is labour intensive, whereas building product manufacturing has more machinery and less labour. An accurate assessment of specific employee space needs has to be completed to evaluate the demand.

### Locality preferences

Certain industries will situate themselves in a specific location due to superior local infrastructure such as services, transport facilities, availability of raw materials and favourable labour conditions. For example, resource industries such as steel need to locate themselves near the mining area. In contrast, the motor manufacturing sector needs to be located close to skilled labour and other complementary component manufacturers.

## Location analysis

When deciding on a location, experienced developers in the industrial field prioritise labour, materials, power, transport, local government policy and local operating cost. On the other hand, industrial centres are primarily market-orientated and, therefore, the decision of where to set up is more determined by transport, prestige and any existing potential for related industries. To find the right locality for developing industrial buildings, you should consider the following variables.

### Population

For this development category, preference should be given to an area that has a population of one million or more with the potential for substantial population and economic growth. However, some industrial developments can operate successfully in areas with a smaller community, particularly if the area boasts the factors discussed below.

### Raw materials

For the industrial manufacturer, the availability of raw materials or complementary value-added services could be a significant deciding factor in where they locate their business.

### Power and fuel

The rates and possible concessions for bulk use of electrical power or fuel by local government or enterprises are seen as a great benefit to a manufacturer.

### Local government policy

Determine the local government policy in terms of tax concessions and economic incentives.

### Labour market

Developers should carefully analyse the local labour market in respect of the availability of a skilled workforce and costs such as wages. Also, review the labour laws, union dominance and productivity output.

### Community

In certain areas, the local community may object to the presence of industry and apply pressure against the development.

### Transportation

Be sure that either an existing highway (or one that is proposed) serves the site. Also, analyse the distance to airports, harbours and railway facilities.

### Related industries

Determine the types of industries that may be moving into the area and the existing ones that have plans for expansion.

### Local operating cost

Analyse the cost of services such as water, sewerage, waste disposal, electricity, transport and other related expenses compared to other locations.

## Site analysis

As well as the location of the development, the following site factors should be analysed in detail.

### Site conditions

Analyse the soil-bearing capacity by examining soil samples. Some industrial-zoned land might be an old landfill area or ex-refuse site. Also evaluate the shape, topography and contours of the land; industrial buildings require large, flat sites, which reduces or eliminates the cost of any excavation or filling of land and the need for retaining walls.

### Zoning

Ensure that the planned or intended use of the proposed industrial building complies with the local structure plan, zoning, easements and any other title restrictions.

### Availability of services

Check the location of the nearest service connections. Extensive distances to water, electricity and sewerage could add significantly to the building budget. Evaluate whether the existing services can suit the requirements of the user.

### Building regulations

Verify the local building regulations regarding health and safety requirements and by-laws. Check all height, building setbacks and fire regulations.

### Environmental restrictions

If the proposed development is designed to accommodate a manufacturer or a processing plant, ensure that the buildings and their use complies with stringent environmental conditions imposed by local, state and federal government agencies.

### Advertising value

A bonus to a developer is if the site provides advertising exposure which can be seen from a major highway or arterial roads.

### Traffic

Analyse whether the existing road system can comfortably accommodate both the movement of large trucks and future volumes of traffic.

## Market profile

The market profiles of individuals or companies who require industrial facilities are:

- National manufacturing companies or large corporations generally want industrial facilities planned and developed for their specific use. The company either develops the facilities themselves or leases them over the long term.
- National distributors such as supermarket chains or the larger department stores require ample warehouse space as well as office facilities, strategically located near sound transport systems and possibly market exposure.
- Investors can be broken into two categories, namely private and institutional. The smaller private investor will be looking for smaller strata-type developments, while institutional investors will be looking for more significant developments with key and stable tenants.
- Small business operators require smaller industrial units for manufacturing or storage. These businesses would look for a strata development to either buy or rent.

## Market analysis

In analysing the market, one must understand the market demand for industrial space, and this can be broken down into 'generated demand' and 'replacement demand'. Generated demand, which represents the greater portion of the market, arises from new companies wishing to locate in a new area or existing companies wanting to expand their operation. Replacement demand is where established companies want to dispose of their obsolete facilities and replace them with superior functional planning, such as good architectural design, better parking, improved trucking manoeuvrability and lower operating costs. The following should be considered in the market analysis.

## Competition

An analysis of the competition should provide essential fundamentals with the marketing strategy such as competitive sale and leasing policies, the range of products on the market and the extent of additional services offered to prospective tenants.

## Employment

An employment analysis, which will establish what changes in employment have occurred in the last ten years and the future trends for the next ten, can, in turn, affect the demand for industrial development.

## Economic base

An economic base analysis is useful in determining the economic base of the local community relative to current economic trends, opportunities and deficiencies. This information will help to identify the types of industrial users that will constitute the most likely sources of demand for industrial space.

## Development team

In large-scale industrial development projects, the development team functions most efficiently when members continually coordinate their respective functions, as documented below:
- architect — an architect is usually required for the minimal aesthetics necessary for the building
- development or project manager — the development or project manager is a pivotal member around which the entire management of the project revolves

- quantity surveyor — quantity surveyors may be required, depending on the project's complexity
- structural engineer — these engineers play a significant role, especially where large roof spans may be required
- civil engineer — this type of engineer should ensure that large transport vehicles can be moved conveniently
- electrical engineer — an electrical engineer would ensure that lighting levels are of a high standard, especially where manufacturing is concerned
- mechanical engineer — a mechanical engineer's involvement will depend on the scale and type of development.

In addition to the key members of the team, specific aspects of the development may require specialist input. Such specialists may include industrial consultants, fire consultants, public relations consultants, geotechnical engineers, environmental scientists and traffic engineers.

## Design considerations

The design of industrial buildings will vary and depend upon several conditions. These conditions may include the operator's specific requirements, the site conditions and, in the case of strata units, the target market. Structural engineers design most industrial buildings because the function of the building is to provide large open spaces. Most industrial buildings house large pieces of machinery, or the tenant requires the layout of the building to be revised to fit their use. Therefore, large open spaces with fewer structural columns are most appropriate as they allow for flexibility and ease of movement. An architect may be involved in the aesthetics and where more complex planning is required.

Regardless, the following design considerations ought to be considered:
- market trends — evaluate the latest trends and technology before creating the brief
- parking — provide adequate parking
- vehicular circulation — provide sufficient space for movement of large trucks and vehicles
- security — provide fences and gates, electronic surveillance systems

- floor to ceiling height — this should be generous (gantries, which are overhead conveying systems that move heavy equipment or material from one area to another, may be required).
- natural lighting — preferably south light (there is less sunlight and glare from the south than the north, east or west, so windows facing south provide more consistent lighting)
- large doors — mainly for smooth movement of forklift trucks
- regulations — check all statutes and building regulations.

## Cost factors

A vital element in a project's feasibility is the development cost estimate. Development costs can vary widely and depend upon factors such as the physical characteristics of the site, the lot size relative to building area and the location and availability of municipal services. Items usually included in the overall costs include:

- land cost — check that the residual factor has been considered
- bulk services — ensure they are adequate
- service and utility connection fees
- construction costs
- development and building plan fees
- development or project manager fees
- holding cost — short construction time and early occupation means less loss of interest
- escalation cost — depending on the size, try to negotiate a fixed contract
- professional fees
- insurances
- levies — transportation and other statutory levies
- external development cost — road widening, for example
- communications
- bank charges and fees
- outgoings — including operating expenses, rates and taxes.

## Marketing

As with office and retail developments, the marketing strategy in industrial developments should be to acquire key tenants, as this makes the development an attractive investment and the project secure in the eyes of institutional financiers.

It is not wise to start the construction of a single-operator industrial building until a tenant has been secured and all lease conditions have been met. The risks are too high, and the developer could be caught with an incomplete building should the tenant fail to meet certain guarantees and conditions.

In a smaller strata development, a certain amount of risk can be taken. Still, it should be conditional upon the developer completing all the necessary market research and being confident that the marketing program will secure the required tenants or that there will be buyers. The marketing program or strategy must be coordinated with the conclusions drawn from the marketing analysis and with the goals of the developer in mind.

## Viability

With all developments, a feasibility study should be undertaken, as well as a sensitivity analysis. Pay attention to the following factors.

### Design and construction

Consultation with a specialist industrial designer is imperative, and such a specialist should have a good understanding of advanced construction techniques that will give the maximum floor area for the minimum total construction cost, therefore improving the viability of the development.

### Outgoings

Consideration should be given to all outgoings even though these may be passed on to the tenant. Some tenants negotiate a lease where the landlord is responsible for part of the operating expenses.

### Returns

Investigate the acceptable returns on such developments in the area you intend developing. If you are providing space for a single, secure national tenant, you may accept a lower return initially but factor in your gain over the long term.

### Phasing

Depending on the size of the development, it makes good business sense that phasing in relation to demand should be taken into consideration. For example, if your proposed development can accommodate 10,000 square metres of building, but the present demand is for 5,000 square metres, you could build the 5,000 square metres in Phase One, and the balance later in Phase Two when the demand increases.

## Tenants

The benefit of investing in an industrial building is that there is likely to be fewer tenants required to fill the building, therefore creating fewer problems for the landlord. Any developer who manages to secure a well-known national tenant will have peace of mind that there will be a stable cash flow for the period of the lease, which is an ideal situation.

When an industrial building is custom-built to a tenant's speci-fication, it is essential to get some background information on the tenant from other people within the same industry — ask questions about their standing and reputation. Additional information can be obtained from industry associations and credit bureaus. It is also a good idea to obtain and check the tenant's references.

## Leases

Like both retail and office leases, industrial real estate leases tend to fall into two bargaining positions: the first is where the tenant is a small company, and the lease is landlord-orientated, while the second is where larger companies negotiate the lease in their favour. However, there are differences between an industrial building lease and other commercial leases, as documented below:

- With industrial developments, the buildings are likely to involve more work to suit tenant requirements.
- As there may be substantial tenant work, industrial real estate leases are more likely to be negotiated on a longer-term.

## Property management

Depending on the size and complexity of the development, a property manager may be required. If you employ a property manager, ensure that the person or company has expertise in industrial buildings, not only with regards to their management skills but also in their network within the industrial community to ensure they have access to possible tenants.

## Conclusion

Of the range of commercial developments, industrial real estate development is one of the more straightforward projects that can be undertaken. Of course, this will depend on the scale and the capital cost involved. Industrial developments should still adhere to the basic principles of real estate development, even though they are not as stimulating as shopping centres.

In most circumstances, you will be dealing with fewer tenants and fewer consultants, therefore taking less of your personal time. These tenants will also take up a reasonably long-term lease, which again makes the package attractive to most investors.

# Chapter 16

# *LAND DEVELOPMENTS*

## Introduction

In contrast to buildings, land cannot be reproduced and depending on its location and site conditions; it can be an increasingly valuable resource. The demand for good quality land can be seen where areas close to a river or beachfront, or sites with excellent views, experience a substantial increase in value.

The benefit of holding vacant land lies in the potential to add value to it. Vacant land can be subdivided or rezoned, and the resulting portions of the land sold for a higher price than the original purchase price, including subdivision or rezoning costs.

Undeveloped land that is not income producing causes the owner to lose the tax benefits usually associated with a developed property. The investor or developer wishing to hold on to undeveloped land should have a substantial cash flow to cover repayments, service charges and the like. Figure 16.1 below is an example of a typical subdivision plan.

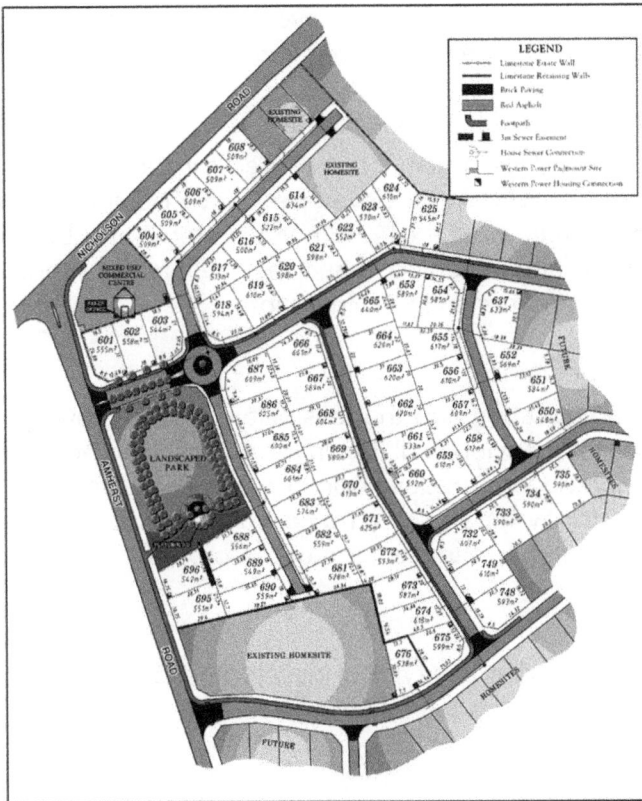

Figure 16.1: Typical subdivision

## Benefits and risks

The benefits and risks include the following.

### Benefits

The benefits of land developments can be rewarding for the following reasons.

*Potential high returns*

As mentioned previously, if the property is well-located, it can become an asset, especially when natural forces such as the increase in population and migration create a demand for new zonings. For example, when rural land is rezoned to urban, the value of the land, which may have been bought at rural land prices, is revalued at a significantly higher rate per square metre.

### Rewards for entrepreneurial effort

Developers with vision can be rewarded for their entrepreneurial effort. For example, some developers have become millionaires overnight by analysing a city's growth patterns and buying large tracts of rural land, rezoning it, and then selling the subdivision as residential and commercial building lots.

### Availability of finance

If the timing, location and the feasibility study is showing a good return, most financiers will be in favour of lending money for vacant land subdivision development, subject to your own financial ability to pay for any holding cost. At times, this finance may be conditional upon the rezoning of the property.

## Risks

The risks involved in this type of development depend mainly on the timing factor, plus the following.

### High holding cost

If the land is bought on a long-term speculative basis, the holding cost can be high, especially if it cannot be rented out for any specific use or before any sale transactions can take place. Delays in rezoning or subdivision approvals can be costly to the developer, as they will be paying interest, land taxes and professional fees without any cash flow or return from the land.

### Extensive government procedures

Any rezoning or subdivision of land attracts several government procedures and can involve local and state departments. Depending on the size and location of the land, some government procedures may require the developer to conduct certain studies such as an environmental impact study, a traffic impact analysis and a social impact study.

*Community approval*

In addition to the standard government approvals, there may be several local active communities and action groups who raise concerns about what impact the rezoning might have on the local inhabitants and the environment. These concerns, if not satisfied, can cause a significant delay in development procedures.

## Development strategy

To be successful in land development, you must continuously be aware of any changes in government planning policies and keep an eye on where urban expansion is taking place. You can achieve this by visiting your State's planning authority and obtaining the latest planning documentation of both present and future policies. By having this information, you have the following options of how to approach your development.

*Speculation*

Speculation can be long-term or short-term. Long-term speculation is to purchase a large tract of rural land and wait for the urban expansion to encroach and then sell. For short-term speculation, you need to be aware of any imminent planning revisions, buy land that will be affected by the changes and sell at the increased value.

*Rezone and sell*

Rezoning and selling involve buying the land as an outright purchase or on an option with certain conditions. Time and effort will need to be spent, ensuring that the rezoning is successful and then in selling the land to another developer who is prepared to erect the buildings.

*Rezone, subdivide and sell*

The strategy of rezoning, subdividing and selling applies mainly to residential or large industrial land lots where the developer completes an overall township plan in conjunction with government planning policy and the long-term structure plans. The application will follow standard government procedures before being sold to various individuals as separate lots.

## Market demand

In previous chapters, we covered the demand for various forms of new real estate developments. Land development is no different and is subject to the same principal market forces.

Successful land development depends on the land's ultimate use, so when analysing the market demand, you should take into consideration the variables associated with specific real estate use. The following list summarises the main variables to be analysed:

- variation in population
- transformation in the economy
- effect of government policies
- changes in the local economic structure
- the availability of land
- new social services.

## Market analysis

In determining the possible buyers of the subdivided lots, conduct market research covering the following areas:

- demographics and consumer profile
- historic sales evidence
- planned infrastructure
- competitors
- sales forecasting
- future profits.

## Location analysis

To find the correct locality for a land development, you will have to spend time researching and keeping up to date with the future planning policies of the State's planning authorities. Your research should also consider the long-term planning of road and rail transport systems and the movement of people closer to employment opportunities.

Avoid environmentally sensitive areas as this could cause undue delay in the rezoning and subdivision applications. Also avoid natural wetlands and land that is low lying, landfill sites such as former rubbish tips, areas with large overhead power lines and land near airports or heavy industrial zones.

When seeking the right location, analyse and consider all the possible potential uses for the land, which may include residential, office, retail or industrial.

## Development team

The team of consultants may vary according to the size of the development, but besides the role of the developer or the development project manager, the three other consultants who play a pivotal part in rezoning and subdivision are the town planner, the civil engineer and land surveyor. Their respective services are listed below:

### Development/project manager

Depending on the scale and complexity of the project, a development manager or project manager with expertise in land development can be appointed to manage and supervise the development process. They will be able to direct the development to ensure its viability so that it can be financed, and the projected returns are achieved.

### Town planner

A town planner is employed from inception to completion, depending on the scale of the project. Their expertise is mainly required in the initial stages, where he or she will conduct several investigations and consultations with various authorities to provide a conceptual masterplan with a proposed subdivision. With the input from other consultants, the planner will provide a detailed structure plan which will be lodged with various authorities for approval. If rezoning is required, the planner will prepare application and motivation documents for council approval.

### Civil engineer

A civil engineer will be required in the initial stages to investigate servicing opportunities and restrictions with relevant authorities. These include the water, electricity and gas authorities, the local authority for development standards of roads and stormwater management, telecommunication service providers, and the government's transport and environmental protection departments. The engineer will inspect the land and investigate the soil and vegetation types, groundwater, existing services, terrain and any other factors that may affect development costs and planning by the town planner.

## Land surveyor

A land surveyor will be used in two stages of the development, namely at the start and at the completion of the project. In the initial stage of the project, the surveyor will prepare a complete survey of the land to be developed, and this will include all existing elements such as trees, water features, services and other distinguishing features. After the completion of the subdivision and approval by various authorities, the surveyor will formalise the subdivision by preparing diagrams and pegging out the subdivided land so that titles can be issued.

## Other consultants

Additional consultants that will be required but may play a lesser role are:

- structural engineer — for retaining walls and bridges
- environmental scientist — for any ecological studies that may be required by various authorities
- geotechnical engineer — for any soil analysis that may be needed for the civil or structural engineer
- anthropologist — used mainly on larger scale projects where he or she would assist and advise the town planner on the social aspects of the community
- architect — for conceptual buildings to show prospective buyers or authorities what the completed product would look like
- landscape architect — for advice on the planting of trees and other vegetation to make the land more attractive
- property valuer — for assistance on the value of the land and subdivision when completed
- real estate agent — for assistance in selling the subdivided land
- advertising and marketing professional — for assistance

with the overall marketing campaign and marketing concepts

- lawyer — for assistance with the drawing up of the sales agreements and any legal matters with authorities or people involved in the project.

## Planning considerations

The design and planning of land development is critical when residential and industrial lots are subdivided in order to be sold. For this exercise, I will concentrate on residential development. Some of the principles applied to residential lots may also be relevant to an industrial subdivision. The following design elements should be considered.

### Lot size and orientation

Throughout the various States in Australia, there is great diversity in the size and orientation of lots. In the past, the standard lot ranged from around 500 to 800 square metres for detached houses. To achieve cost efficiency, there are now several local authorities encouraging a range of lot sizes ranging from 400 to 450 square metres or less. Australian households are getting smaller, and lifestyles are changing so that more time is spent on leisure activities away from home. As a result, homeowners do not have as much time to maintain a big garden. When designing for smaller lots, the planning team should, where relevant, consider the following factors:

- the natural contours and orientation of the land and soil conditions
- the need to retain special features such as trees and views
- the efficient cost of providing new and existing services
- the need to avoid unnecessary repetition
- the ability to facilitate energy conservation through correct solar orientation.

### Built form

The final design and planning of homes or buildings on each lot is not part of a land developer's financial feasibility. Still, it will be beneficial to the marketing strategy to consider the following design factors:

- scale, height and density of the homes
- overall housing theme or character
- provision of privacy, natural light and energy conservation
- building lines and various setbacks
- provision of private open space
- vehicle parking.

Planning guidelines should allow enough on-site space for resident's and visitor's cars and residential streets to be kept free of parked vehicles to prevent road obstructions or traffic hazards. Guidelines and planning requirements can be found in the various local planning schemes.

## Streetscape

The design and character of the streetscape in a residential land subdivision is essential in determining the value and image of the properties. It also contributes significantly to neighbourhood identity. The following factors contribute to the value of a street-scape

- quality of formal and informal landscaping
- retention of natural vegetation and existing trees
- use of natural features and terrain
- design of street paving and verge widths
- control and design of street furniture such as light poles and signs
- control of architectural styles
- design and control of the height and material of fences.

## Transport networks

During the preparation of the overall conceptual site layout, the design team should start with the most sensitive elements of transportation, which are the needs of pedestrians and cyclists. The major routes should follow easy gradients and should link residential areas with schools, open spaces and community activity centres. The layout of possible bus routes and the development of the street network should be considered as well. As a rule, traffic volumes and speeds should be minimised on streets within the residential zone for reasons of safety, the impact of traffic movement and noise.

## Street design

Besides the overall transport network, the design team should take special care with the detail and design of the street layout and consider factors such as:

- street reserve width (area reserved for future road widening) and pavement width
- sightlines (clear vision lines for vehicles approaching intersections) and distances
- street and pavement markings and design
- turning circles to accommodate refuse and fire trucks
- provisions for public transport
- street furniture, including street lighting
- provisions for pedestrians and cyclists.

The provision of facilities for pedestrians and cyclists must be an integral part of the design of the total transportation network. All residents should have the opportunity to walk or cycle to community facilities. Designing for the safety of children, disabled and aged persons is particularly essential, especially where they must cross a busy street.

## Services

The servicing of residential subdivision developments includes the provision of water supply, sewerage, electricity, gas, telephone and stormwater, which are usually provided through a series of underground ducts, either within the road reserve or at the rear of a lot. Separate authorities control these utilities, and in the past, no attempt has been made to combine installation, other than an agreed location for each service. More recently, efforts have been made for sharing trenches, which provides the following advantages:

- cost-effectiveness with fewer trenches and less construction
- accurate location of services for maintenance and repairs
- reduced verge width and disturbance
- earlier settlement and reinstatement (that is, repairing the damage made by other contractors).

### Public open space

Local authorities usually stipulate the absolute minimum open space required to ensure that enough area is planned at the design stage. More recently, the ongoing maintenance of these spaces has become a concern for the local authorities so when planning areas for open space it is important to balance the actual and future use against its ongoing maintenance requirements.

# Rezoning

Rezoning a property from its present use to a zoning that is of higher commercial value can present substantial financial rewards on astute developers who have the vision and motivation to see their ideas come to fruition. For example, this can be achieved by acquiring a vacant piece of land zoned residential and rezoning it to a shopping area. This new zoning will attract a higher market value than if the land had remained residential. However, this is easier said than done, as there will be several difficulties the developer will encounter, as described below.

### Restrictions

Restricting zoning is how governments can regulate and control the specific use of land. The reason for these zonings is the promotion of health, safety and welfare in the interest of the public. Zoning laws should not be arbitrary, unreasonable or discriminatory, and they should be clear, specific and easily understood by the public.

### Granting of rezoning

When granting a rezoning to an existing town planning scheme, local authorities are required to consider the following factors:
- whether the proposed alternative zoning will be consistent with the general character of the surrounding area
- whether the proposed alternative zoning is socially desirable to the neighbourhood and the surrounding areas
- whether the applicant's motivation is personal or in the interest of the public.

**Strategy to obtain rezoning.**

The applicants who are most successful in obtaining rezoning approval work on their presentation (detailed drawings and written documents to support rezoning) and strategy rather than just on the pure benefits of the scheme. It is achieved by being knowledgeable about factors affecting rezoning applications, including:

- Mistrust — it is regrettable but true that the residents generally do not trust developers. It is mainly due to unscrupulous developers of the past. Your development proposals will usually be introducing new people into the neighbourhood, changing the environment and altering traffic flows. All these changes arouse fears, with residents sometimes objecting to any proposal without analysing the merits of the development.
- Local politics — be aware that local politics may become involved and that local councillors will have specific views on certain issues. You should find out what these views or ideals are and orientate your presentation towards solving or avoiding these issues.
- Public costs — any rezoning will create new public costs, such as essential services and additional motor traffic. Your presentation must convince all concerned that your proposal will benefit the neighbourhood and will not create unnecessary burdens upon the community.
- Different viewpoints — appreciate the fact that the local planning authorities, interest groups and residents will have differing views to your own. It may help to consult with these groups before the formal submission of your application. The presentation of your proposal should constructively answer any concerns voiced by these various bodies.

## Cost factors

While the preliminary cost of land subdivision development may be like other developments, the breakdown of the construction cost will differ, as there are no buildings involved. Listed below are the costs that must be considered when undertaking a feasibility study in a land subdivision development:

- land purchase
- rezoning
- subdivision
- bulk services
- construction cost
- holding cost
- escalation cost
- development manager fees
- professional consulting fees
- insurance
- levies — transportation and other statutory levies
- external development cost — road widening
- advertising and marketing
- finance charges and fees

## Finance

The approval of finance for a subdivision land development will depend mainly on the feasibility study but more importantly, the stage of the development and upon the cash flow of the project in line with the planned stages or phases. Financial institutions should be approached in the early stages of the project so that they can get a feeling for the project as the development concept progresses.

Before seeking finance, at least have the following information to present:
- historical background of the land and surrounding areas
- a description of the project and any distinctive qualities
- a valuation report of the property
- details of the market research conducted
- details of the development company and shareholders
- details of the borrower's financial position

## Construction

Once tender procedures have been followed through, and a civil contractor has been appointed to carry out the construction work, the process for the clearance of the subdivision should start.

The appointed civil engineer should arrange inspections with various authorities to check that installation of all the necessary services, including the earthworks, roads and stormwater drains, is satisfactory. All construction work should be in accordance with the approved drawings and any other conditions of approval by the relevant authorities.

As soon as the works are completed, 'as constructed' drawings should be submitted for the issue of certificates of title. Bear in mind that the contractor's obligations are not fulfilled until a 12month maintenance period has passed. The contract should allow for 2.5 per cent of the contract sum to be retained, which is released at the end of the maintenance period.

## Marketing

Depending on the size of the development and the designated budget, you may decide to do 'in-house' marketing or employ professional consultants such as real estate agents. The marketing exercise should aim to promote a specific community lifestyle through various forms of media such as newspapers, radio, brochures and other forms of media.

The start of the marketing program will depend on a strategy devised from the earlier research completed. Factors that drive a marketing program are:

- whether pre-sales are part of the conditions for financing the start of the project
- the present state of the market and competition
- whether the marketing research shows that consumers need to see the completed project before committing themselves.

In addition to the above, there are alternative marketing strategies, which successful land developers have adopted in the past.

### Limited release

Employing the limited release strategy means that the development will be released in stages. Each stage has only a limited number of lots and, invariably, there are more buyers than lots available which creates a 'must buy' mentality before the price increases at the next stage. The success of this strategy will depend on the prevailing market conditions.

### Display homes

Most new land developments will have several lots at the entrance to the development available to project builders. It has a twofold benefit, as it creates an established look and generally project builders spend a great deal of money on their own advertising, thus attracting large groups of potential buyers to the land.

### Incentives

Several incentives can be employed to attract buyers, such as free fencing or landscaping, or a cash discount on early completion of a buyer's new home.

### Developer finance

Having the developer's financier offering finance to potential buyers will assist the developer, the buyer and the financier. They would have already valued the land and would possibly provide better terms and conditions to purchasers.

## Conclusion

Having read this chapter, you are now probably thinking, 'Why build or develop a real estate? Why not sell land as it stands?' There are two reasons why land should be improved:

1. A substantially developed property is worth considerably more than a property that has not been developed.
2. A developed property produces an income with tax benefits, whereas a vacant site costs money to maintain.

Some developers specialise only in developing land. These developers set out long-term plans and development strategies and purchase semi-rural property three to five years (or more) before the urban creep reaches their investment. To do the same, you would need a reasonable amount of money to sustain this period of negative income and have the patience to wait for the anticipated windfall.

# Chapter 17

# OTHER FORMS OF REAL ESTATE DEVELOPMENTS

## Introduction

Development types can be categorised into three main areas, namely residential, commercial and community or what I term as social infrastructure. For example, under residential, there are retirement villages, residential aged care, golf course estates and student housing. Commercial developments include hotels and resorts, serviced apartments, commercial parking facilities, entertainment centres, theme parks, conference centres, self-storage and many more. While under community, there are childcare centres, education facilities, medical centres, community centres and sporting venues.

The last few chapters covered the more notable forms of real estate development types, namely residential and commercial highlighting key points to consider. In this chapter, I broadly include other forms of developments opportunities that do not come around very often. Armed with the knowledge of the basic structure and elements of these alternative developments helpful. It may provide you with an opportunity to fill in a market that is untapped in your area or they could become part of a mixed-use development.

To cover each of these alternative asset types and their particularities would need another book. However, I have selected a few of the more topical developments that you may encounter during your development career. These include senior's accommodation, student housing, childcare centres and hotels and resorts.

## Seniors Accommodation

In Australia, there is a variety of senior's accommodation. These include retirement villages, manufactured home villages, rental villages, over 55's villages, lifestyle villages, lifestyle communities, lifestyle estates, retirement resorts and residential aged care or nursing homes. In breaking them into groups, three primary forms of senior's accommodation are offered to seniors.

### Types of senior accommodation

Under senior's accommodation, there is a variety of facilities that cater to our older generation who have reached the retirement age, and these include.

- *Independent retirement living communities*
  Independent retirement living communities, also known as retirement villages, is restricted to seniors who are over 55 years or have retired from full-time employment. Most villages offer residents the choice of Independent Living Units (commonly referred to as an 'ILU' or 'villa') or serviced apartment accommodation. These units are designed for the independent, active retiree who does not require assistance with day-to-day living. Many villages provide dining services, basic housekeeping, laundry services, transport to appointments, activities, social programs, and access to exercise equipment. Some also offer emergency panic alarm systems, live-in managers, and amenities like pools, spas, clubhouses, and on-site beauty and hair salons.

- *Retirement Lifestyle Communities*
  Retirement lifestyle communities, also known as manufactured home villages, are for those over 50 years of age. These developments are similar to a retirement village. Instead of an on-site building, the units are single-level transportable homes. These communities also include some communal leisure facilities for its residents and may incorporate on-site health or medical services. Some communities are exclusively for permanent residents, while others accommodate a combination of permanent residents and short-term holidaymakers.

- *Residential Aged Care*
  Residential aged care is for older people who can no longer live at home. Services provide continuous supported care ranging from help with daily tasks and personal care to 24-hour nursing care. The Commonwealth Government is responsible for the provision of residential aged care services and regulates the quality of care standards and funding under the Aged Care Act 1997. Residential aged care services are delivered by a range of providers including not-for-profit, private and public sector organisations.

For this exercise and to get a broad overview of this sector, I will cover developing independent retirement villages.

## Demand for retirement accommodation

The outlook for senior's accommodation developments is positive, with increasing activity and market uptake in the medium term. It is due to the following factors.

- *Rapidly growing retiree population:*
  Between 2018 and 2055 the total Australian population is projected to grow from 24.9 million to 39.4 million. It equates an increase of 14.5 million or 65% over the 36 years. Senior Australians aged 65 years and above will more than double from 3.6 million to 8.5 million over this period.

- *Life expectancy increasing as the population ages:*
  With the improvements in medical science, life expectancy is rising. In 2015 the life expectancy averaged around 80 years for a male and 84 years for a female. It is projected to increase to between 87 years and 88 years for males and females respectively by 2055.

- *Health care cover:*
  In the 1970s, over 75% of the population had medical insurance cover. Still, with the introduction of private health insurance in 1975 and Medicare in 1984, insurance levels fell. The Medicare Levy surcharge increased in 2008, and the 30% rebate means testing from July 2012 saw private health insur-

ance rise to 47% in 2014, higher than other countries such as the UK with only 14% coverage.

- *Greater Government spend on the older generation:*
  Starting from birth, government spending peaks at an average $31,690 per person p.a. for the 5 to 9 age group. With the age pension, there is a jump in government spending in health and aged care. When residents reach 70 - 74 spending per person p.a. rises to $32,568 and 90 - 94 it is $72,630, which is 4.7 times greater than spending on a person aged in the 20 - 24 age group.

- *Government spending on health and aged care to increase:*
  In 2015-16 Government spending, which includes disability, social security, welfare, and defence spending, accounted for 43% of total government spending. While all retiree-related expenditure (health care, aged pension, and aged care) accounting for 37%. Over the next 45 years all retiree-related spending will grow proportionally and monetary terms, increasing to over half (52%) of total government spending.

### Developing Independent Retirement Villages

Developing an independent retirement community or retirement village is like developing a group housing villa-style project or an apartment block. From a design level, the critical difference is ensuring that all buildings are designed to universal standards, i.e. for wheelchair accessibility. Depending on the size and scale of the project, there may be communal facilities like dining, club lounges, library etc. included in the project. Depending on the developer, the ownership and management structure may be different if the units are not sold under a strata title.

### Site location

The suitability of a development site and its surroundings for retirement homes must be carefully examined before embarking on a project. The level of demand for this specialised form of housing should be ascertained, and the suitability of the locality should be carefully considered. In both publicly funded and privately financed developments, the proximity of peer groups, family and friends is essential. The criteria for site selection are considered below:

- *Demographics*
  The market for retirement housing is not unlimited, so the existence of demand should be firmly established.

- *Communal and leisure facilities*
  For the convenience of day-to-day living, there must be easy access to post office, bank, shops, health centre, church, community centre, library, adult education centre and leisure facilities.

- *Transport*
  Pedestrian routes to service and leisure facilities are essential. Five hundred metres from the site to these areas is about the maximum acceptable distance. The site location must not be such that roads with heavy vehicular traffic have to be crossed to reach shops and other local facilities.

## Retirement village contracts

The tenure for retirement villages is subject to legislation which varies from State to State and in conjunction with operator preference. The more common types of contracts for retirement villages are a long-term lease and strata title. Other arrangements include company title, unit trust, and periodic tenancy. Retirement village operators utilise a range of different financial structures and ownership models as follows:

- *Long-term lease:*
  There are several lease variations across Australia with similar characteristics. Residents are provided with a long-term lease contract, e.g. for life or 99 years, with the right to use common areas and the village facilities. The resident pays an ingoing contribution and pay a maintenance fee, usually on a monthly or quarterly basis. In some retirement villages, this charge is a fixed percentage of the age pension. The more common lease is the "lease for life" with a deferred management fee (DMF). The resident would purchase a of a home unit but is charged

the DMF when they sell or leave the village.

- *Strata title ownership.*
  Strata title is a typical contract offered by retirement village developers seeking to make a profit. The resident pays the agreed purchase price, which includes GST to the developer, whereby the resident occupies the premises and become a member of the owner's corporation. The resident will be registered as the owner of the unit with title deed held at the Land Titles Office. They will also have to pay owners corporation fees while they own the unit.

## The pros of retirement homes

- *Growing demand* - There is a growing demand for retirement accommodation, especially in the affordable sector, whether for sale or rent.
- *Largest market* - The baby boomer market is the largest, fastest-growing target market within the seniors living spectrum.
- *Less competition* - There are very few options that exist for retirees to rent accommodation which give specialist developers more opportunities.
- *Lack of supply* - Due to the high demand for affordable retirement accommodation in this growing sector, there is a lack of new supply coming onto the market.
- *Government subsidies* - For affordable senior's housing, rental income is underpinned by the Federal Government given that most residents are eligible for rental assistance.

## The cons of retirement homes

- *Funding more complex* - Funding from banks is not as easy as regular residential, and most lenders do not have a good understanding of this sector.
- *Limited secondary market* - The secondary resale market is limited and generally only open to other retirees. Most retirement projects have a specific age bracket who could reside within its premises.
- *Limited rental options* - Rental units located in retirement villages are currently the only viable option for the average

investor to access direct property exposure to the retirement sector. It poses a higher risk than standard residential property.

## Tips on developing Seniors Accommodation

Senior's accommodation developments can be a lucrative business. However, it takes knowledge, experience, and financial resources to successfully undertake these developments. Below are tips that will assist:

- *Have a reliable financial partner*
  Having a partner with substantial financial capital can play a significant role in these developments, especially when starting this type of development.

- *Assemble an experienced development team*
  Seniors accommodation development projects require a development team that has specialised knowledge and experience in this sector. Expertise in building, legal, property management and financing experts will assist in lessening mistakes during the development process.

- *Find government land*
  Land for senior's accommodation can be expensive. However, as these developments provide a social need to the community, it is worthwhile seeking government-owned land at a lower cost than commercially priced property.

- Work with experienced operators
  Experienced operators can provide guidance and knowledge of the type of senior's project undertaken. They can point out design and planning issues that will make their management and operation of the development a lot smoother.

# Student Accommodation

Historically, higher-learning institutions developed and managed their on-campus housing operations. Over the past 20 years, new universities and tertiary colleges have had significant growth. Unfortunately, the provision of student accommodation has not kept up the expansion. In Australia, one of the significant factors contributing to this growth is the influx of overseas students. Over the past two decades, the number of international students coming to Australia have increased, creating a \$15 billion industry. In many instances, education centres have outsourced student housing development for several reasons; reduced public and private funding; increased expectations for building amenities; pressure to provide quality facilities quickly; and interest in leveraging resources, mainly cost and availability of capital.

## Types of Student Housing

Student housing can be split into two main categories, namely On-campus and Off-campus, with some sub-categories.

## On-Campus

- *Institutional*
  These are traditional buildings developed by the university or college and are part of the campus. The administration and management of these buildings are under the control of the institution.

- *Leasing*
  Under this scheme, a university or college leases land within the campus to a private developer who will build, operate and administer the buildings for the term of the lease.

## Off-Campus

- *Shared Housing*
  It is where students group together to rent a property or go into an established household offered by working people, students or families. The bedroom provided may be furnished or unfurnished with use of the other household areas and facilities.

- *Renting*
  Vacant properties vary from one to four or more bedrooms. Most vacant apartments, units and houses are unfurnished except for fully self-contained 'granny' flats or bungalows and holiday houses.

- *Off-Campus Residences*
  There are some Residences in the community operated by private providers. Residences offer furnished bedrooms and equipped common areas. Rental includes all expenses such as gas and electricity typically unless rooms are separately metered.

- *Full Board 5 and 7 days*
  Usually includes a fully furnished room, breakfast and dinner and utility costs included in a set price. Lunch, laundry and other services may be negotiated or offered by the provider.

## Market Demand

The financial pressures and influx of overseas students on universities and colleges have led to the trend to outsource student accommodation on campus. As universities and colleges come to view student housing as an operating business, this creates opportunities for partnerships with private developers to meet student accommodation needs.

Since the early 1980s, the quality of Australian education has become better known and promoted more widely internationally. As the economies of Asian countries grew, so did their need for a skilled, educated workforce. Australia absorbed many students who might otherwise have studied in the United States or the United Kingdom because Asian students perceived it as being closer and cheaper.

## Location Analysis

The increased demand has resulted in the establishment of 'niche' student markets.

- *Clusters*
  With the high demand from students for private rented accommodation, there is a tendency for students to 'cluster' in specific areas. It is because students prefer to live close to their institution to minimise travel costs. Locations close to the city centre are popular with students for the nightlife and part-time work opportunities.

- *Niche leasing*
  A vital characteristic of the student market is 'niche leasing'. Investors move into student areas to target this segment of the market. In many instances will consult with the university or college on students' requirements regarding the locality, size, and type of accommodation, and rent level, which can be charged.

- *Low demand areas*
  In low demand areas, investors offer not only safe and well-maintained housing. In many cases they also provide amenities such as microwave cookers and satellite TV to attract students.

- *High demand areas*
  In high demand areas, students are willing to live in more mediocre quality accommodation to save money or to be in what was the right area. It is also evident that poor conditions were caused or exacerbated by the students. For example, students not disposing of rubbish properly, or by not cleaning or ventilating cooking areas adequately.

**Development viability**

The viability of a student residence and its facilities requires an in-depth analysis that goes beyond the typical analysis required for similar income-producing properties, such as hotels and motels. Most developers pursuing student-housing aim to secure a healthy rental return. While others may develop, operate and then sell to a group or individual investors. Whether developers hold or sell the bottom line is that the project must prove to be viable. It should show good rental returns not only when completed but also in the long-term.

One of the aspects of the future viability of a student housing project is to anticipate the demand fifteen to twenty years away accurately. Many institutions of higher education may have future projections relating to enrolments. One of the most accurate methods in evaluating next admission and demand is to examine current enrolment statistics among kindergarten and elementary school students. This information can be gathered from state and federal education offices.

## Pros of student housing

- *Growing demand*
  The expansion of the higher education sector has taken place with minimal attention given to shelter the growing student population. Accommodation provision by the higher education institutions has not grown commensurately with student numbers.

- *Reliable income*
  Compared to other residential investments, developers and investors target this market as they see students as reliable tenants, and as being good at paying the rent on time.

- *Higher returns*
  Unlike other parts of the residential sector, the student rental market appears to be robust. Developers and investors can often achieve higher profits from leasing a shared house for several students than can be obtained from renting other types of household.

- *Less sophistication*
  As most students are itinerant and are on usually short-term leases, they do not develop an emotional attachment to their accommodation. Therefore, developers do not have to provide sophisticated finishes to attract the student market.

## Cons of student housing

- *Oversupply*
  Like all asset classes, the student housing market can be subject to oversupply. It can lead to empty properties that are not readily available to other renting groups. It can be attributed to investor's leasing preferences or because other groups do not seek accommodation in the 'student areas'. Competition between investors for student households could push up standards of amenity.

- *Poor location*
  Areas further away from the educational institution will increase the cost of travel for students. Preferable places would be near education centres or where students congregate.

- *Short-term leases*
  Some students only want a short-term lease or rental option for nine months or less. These are mainly rural, interstate and international students who often prefer to return home for the summer break.

- *Limited market segment*
  Other groups, such as young professionals and low-income households, tended not to compete for the same properties as students. It, therefore, limits the development to students only.

## Tips on developing student housing

A feasibility study and market assessment should be your first step in planning a new student housing development. This study will help you gain an understanding of the student population and the competition, including both current and projected growth in campus enrolment and housing supply. In addition to this study, it is helpful to acknowledge the following:

- *Use sustainability as a driver*
  This trend follows a broader move toward environmental sensitivity in all university construction. Students, faculty, and donors all seem to unite behind the idea of sustainable design. School administrators also see cost advantages in thinking green.

- *Get to know the local student market*
  Universities publish student demographics specific to their campus. This data varies in-depth and often fails to offer enough market-specific data to guide unit mix and amenity planning adequately. Primary research on students at your target teaching institution is typically required to complement the available secondary data.

- *Plan the right unit mix and amenity*
  The right amenity packages and unit mix will increase a project's leasing potential. While pools and fitness rooms are standard amenities, insights gained directly from student population should inform the need and potential usage of other facilities.

- *Evolve with technology*
  With practically every student carrying around multiple wireless devices, communities quickly realise it is no longer strictly about bandwidth. Add to this, the total number of numerous personal device connections and the overall requirements are rapidly expanding.

- *Build vertical*
  Even when buying more land is a possibility, choosing to build up and not out makes sense. Consider the advantages of student housing that is anywhere from five to 30 stories high. This approach influences cost.

- *Introduce micro-housing*
  One of the prevailing trends in student housing is micro-housing. Instead of the older two-bed dorm room approach, students are provided with small spaces set up for sleeping, studying, and preparing simple meals. Freeing up square meterage ensures that the common areas can be larger and more user-friendly.

- *Consider modular design*
  With the repetition of room sizes with built-in furniture and fittings, modular design and construction should be considered. Besides the cost savings in the duplication of product and construction time factory constructed modular units have sustainable values due to less material wastage.

## Childcare Centres

Childcare, or otherwise known as daycare, is the care and supervision of a child or multiple children at a time-aged from six weeks to thirteen years. Some strong trends are driving growth in the childcare centre industry, which includes stable government funding, growing demand for locations and the increase in workforce participation. A significant part of the cash flow of childcare centres is Government sourced. The move from the current rebate or benefits system to the new subsidy system will increase the funding available for lower-income families.

## Types of Childcare Centres

The size and facilities of childcare centres vary according to the number of children attending and the type of services offered by the operator. Most childcare centres in older suburbs are home conversions. In contrast, new centres are being developed in either newly established suburbs or part of a mixed-use development. The services offered by most operators include:

- *Long Day Care:*
  This service provides all-day care or part-time care for children, usually below school age. It is the most popular form of childcare, and it has had steady growth over the last five years. There is a heavy reliance for this service by parents, particularly for children below the age of 4 years.

- *Family Day Care:*
  Educators provide a flexible care arrangement and developmental activities in their own homes for children on behalf of an approved Family Day Care service. This segment is popular within regional areas and has seen significant growth in the past seven years.

- *Occasional Day Care:*
  It mainly caters for the needs of families who require short term care for their children, which are usually non-school aged. The service is flexible according to community needs by providing care at short notice and in emergencies.

- *Outside School Hours Care:*
  This care is for school going aged children providing care before or after school during the school term. As parents are working longer, the number of children in this segment grows. It also includes vacation care (childcare services during school holidays) which is becoming more popular, adding further demand for outside school hours' care services.

## The childcare market

With population growth forecast over the next five years' and maternal participation rates, the demand in the childcare sector will grow further. The demand for new centres will grow exponentially due to the Australian Government's focus on providing affordable and accessible childcare services. The key drivers of this market include:

- *More women in the workforce.*
  Today more women are employed in the workforce than in the past plus the number of women to go back to work after giving birth. It has presented a long-term opportunity as more families use childcare services resulting in more investment in this sector.

- *Increased demand*
  In 2010, there were about 5,900 long daycare centres nationwide, but now there are well over 6,800. The figures in before and after-school care, and short-term daycare have also risen.

- *Government support*
  As the costs of these services increase, so too has government support. The Federal Government first introduced subsidy payments for childcare in the early 1970s. Today, 50 years later, with the Government's ongoing financial support has transformed this sector with over 1.2 million children attend an estimated 17,000 government-approved childcare services nationwide.

- *Secure future*
  Childcare creates additional benefits for the community, securing the industry's future. These benefits include better socialisation, the transition to school, and improved performance in the early years of primary school.

**Site Selection**

Selecting an appropriate site is one of the critical challenges in developing a new childcare centre. A childcare centre is a regulated business that must comply with specified design requirements to obtain a license to operate. There is no unique formula in identifying a site for a childcare centre. Still, as a rule of thumb, it is wise to look at all possible avenues which can include:

- *Use existing contacts for potential sites*
  These contacts include schools, religious organisations, neighbourhood groups and local and state Government. Community or public sites are more likely to be lower in cost than commercial land.

- *Stand-alone or part of a mix-use*
  Decide early whether you want an independent centre or whether you would like to be part of a mixed-use development. Typical site options include (a) independent commercial site or (b) a site in community facilities, such as a church, school or multi-purpose social service centre.

- *Co-locate with new housing or mixed-use projects.*
  To identify potential sites and partners, you should contact your local housing community or government agencies that finance community or affordable housing development.

## The pros in childcare centres

- *Long term lease:*
  Childcare centres offer long term leases with most terms ranging from 15 to 20 years with options and an average of 3 per cent annual rental increase.

- *Strong yields:*
  The childcare industry has historically recorded higher yields compared to office, retail and industrial sectors. Yields range from 6 per cent to 10 per cent, which has outstripped all other real estate asset classes.

- *Payment of outgoings:*
  Under the lease agreements, the operators are responsible for paying the property taxes, insurance but maintenance items and repairs are the landlord's responsibility.

- *Government support:*
  The Australian Government aims to incentivise families to return to work by increasing accessibility to childcare services.

- *Steady demand:*
  The increasing demand is underpinned by steady population growth as well as the female workforce participation rates, which have been on a consistent upturn since the 1980s.

- *Tenant investments:*
  Tenants invest heavily in their properties, leading to fewer relocations, longer-term leases, and higher levels of income stability.

## The cons in childcare centres

- *Poor location:*
  The success of a childcare centre is highly dependent on its location and the catchment area. Selecting a site in the wrong address can lead to business failure.

- *Poor operator:*
  As an owner of the childcare centre building, you want to ensure that the operator you contract to lease the property has a good track record. Poor performance by the operator may lead to the delay in lease payments or finding a new operator should their business fail.

- *Low capital growth:*
  Like most commercial real estate investments, capital growth is more moderate than residential real estate as the value is linked to the lease agreement between the building owner and the tenant operator.

## Tips on developing childcare centres

- *Find an experienced operator*
  Experienced operators with a good track record can provide income stability and facilitate the financing of a new centre. They can also assist with design and planning issues for smoother management.

- *Find a location with less competition*
  With support from the Government, there are a significant number of new childcare centres springing up in older suburbs.

Therefore, research the area and analyse the competition to see if there is potential for another player in the area.

- *Check zoning with the council*
Most childcare centres are located within a residential area, so it is essential that you should check the zoning with the local council. If not, ask the planning officer if the council would support a childcare centre on the proposed site and what the process is in changing its current use.

- *Find a corner site*
Corner sites have better exposure and accessibility due to having two street frontages. Before committing to purchase the property, check with the local council if the proposed access and egress will be acceptable.

## Hotels and resorts

Developing a hotel or a resort starting from initiating the concept, finding the ideal location, selecting a brand segment and obtaining financing is an exciting and fulfilling exercise. However, it comes with significant challenges to achieve financial success, not only in the short term but also in its future operations. It is not one for the faint-hearted. Before you venture into any of these developments, you must make strategic planning a priority. One solution to ease the process is to find a credible hotel brand with extensive expertise who can support you in your development strategy. This brand partner can provide a distinct advantage and is a powerful driver of hotel development during the development process. Therefore, find an industry frontrunner with a strong presence in the hospitality industry. Find one that keeps its brands with innovative marketing, one that is on top of new technology and values developer brand loyalty and growth. Taking this path will ease the pain of learning about the industry and avoids making mistakes along the way.

### Types of hotels

By definition, a hotel building has a minimum of six bedrooms with at least three having an ensuite bathroom. Hotels can be classified into 'Star' categories ranging from a single Star up to six

Stars. From an international aspect, there is no standard method of assigning these Stars and compliance with common requirements is voluntary. Hotels vary in the type of services targeted at specific markets. These can be classified according to the following markets:

- *Business hotels:*
  These are the largest group of hotel types, and they primarily cater to business travellers and usually located within the central business districts. Although they mainly serve business travellers, they also provide for individual tourists, group tourist and small conference groups.

- *Resort hotels:*
  Resort hotels are generally located in a tourist area or an exotic location outside of a metropolitan area or city and used for relaxation or recreation, attracting visitors for holidays or vacations. Depending on their location, they provide recreational facilities such as golf, tennis, sailing, skiing and swimming.

- *Airport hotels:*
  These hotels are located close or adjacent to airports and typically targets business guests, airline passengers with overnight travel or cancelled flights and airline crews or staff. Some Airport hotels also charge by the hour instead of standard daily night charges.

- *Medi-hotels:*
  These hotels are located close to or within the grounds of a hospital. They provide accommodation and hotel services for self-caring patients accessing acute hospital services. As a substitute for multi-day admitted inpatient care, a Medi-hotel assist the transition between the public and acute care plus help patients to access hospital services.

- *Casino hotels:*
  Hotels located adjacent or part of a gambling facility are known as Casino Hotels. Although the food and beverage offerings in the casino are luxurious, their functions are secondary to and supportive of casino operations.

- *Boutique hotels:*
  These hotels are not part of a brand with a chain of hotels. They feature an intimate and stylish design and provide excellent amenities. These hotels are small, ranging from 6 rooms to less 100 rooms.

## Market profile

In running a successful hospitality accommodation business, it is essential to understand the needs. It includes your guests' preferences and the various segments of these guest. For business planning, it is necessary to understand the profile of these tourist segments and to draw distinctions between them as described below.

*Business Tourists:*

It includes people travelling for business reasons, including attending conferences or exhibitions and business meetings.

- *Location is essential:* Business travellers are always pressed for time as their schedules are packed with meetings and presentations, which makes a hotel's location a top priority. Therefore, a convenient location that is close to their meeting s or conference is vitally important.

- *The need to be connected:* Businesspeople are extensively using their mobile phone or to remain connected with their clients and colleagues during their business trips. Access to their email is essential.

- *Loyalty programs:* Due to the high frequency of travel and less time spent on bookings, business tourists tend to stick with specific accommodation that matches their criteria. Offering a loyalty program with special offers such as free upgrades or free services is a great way to keep business tourists returning.

- *All-inclusive amenities:* Hotels that provide all the necessary facilities that business tourists need to prepare for their work in the morning is of great importance. Amenities like breakfast, a coffee machine, ironing board and services are essential. After a working day, business tourists like to unwind, so offering them a free drink in the lounge area and having a stocked minibar will be attractive.

## Leisure Tourists

These are tourists visiting various places for pleasure or for general interest or just taking a much-needed holiday.

- *Price sensitive:* Compared to business travellers who generally spend more on their travels, leisure tourists tend to be more price-sensitive. Leisure tourists spend more time deciding on the most suitable hotel for their journey and make a significant effort to find the best possible deal.

- *Keen on reviews and recommendations:* Leisure tourists refer to their family, friends, and online reviews when deciding where to stay for their holidays. Any poor recommendations or negative reviews remove a hotel or resort from their selection. Therefore, it is imperative for operators to regularly respond to reports and resolve issues that are presented to them.

- *Attracted to specials and package deals:* Leisure tourists are always looking out for any special offers or package deals. With the mindset of having a great vacation experience, most leisure tourists are looking for accommodation that offers them incentives to stay with them.

- *Extra on-site hotel facilities:* Leisure tourists are attracted to extra "frills" that holiday accommodation can provide them. A hotel or resort that has a pool, gymnasium and a good restaurant is a boost to attract them. So, if your business mix is mostly comprised of leisure tourists, it is beneficial to highlight your hotel's additional facilities and amenities.

## Specific tourist

This category includes sportspeople, sports fans, religious groups and any other groups that are travelling because of specific needs.

- *Location near the venue:* The location to this sector is vital as moving groups of tourists around can be a logistical nightmare. Hospitality accommodation close to a sports stadium for sports fans and near a convention centre for tourist attending a three-day conference will capture most of these guests.

- *Group discounts:* Understandably, the organisers for this sector will be seeking the best discounts on offer from accommodation providers. For example, specific airlines would have a set discount with an accommodation provider for the pilots and flight attendants for overnight accommodation based on the volume of airline staff frequenting their hotel.

- *Travel packages:* International group tours organised by travel agents will often offer tour packages to tourist visiting another country or state. Often these packages include stays over a few days with a specific accommodation provider.

## Pros in hotels and resorts

Developing hospitality accommodation has many benefits to those willing to tackle this challenging development. Below are some of the pros:

- *High returns*
  The developer is rewarded if the timing of the development falls within the market cycle together with the right location. During its operation period, there is a higher cash flow and further capital growth when sold after its third year of operation, which is known as the stabilised year.

- *Modern trends*
  With the continual changing trends in the hospitality accommodation industry, new buildings with trendy décor and architecture will always be more attractive to a guest. Hotels or resorts that do not upgrade their premises to keep in line with new trends will tend to lose their appeal and attract less guest.

- *International branding*
  An internationally recognised hotel or resort brand will always have a higher occupation rate than a lesser-known local brand. The reason for this is that well-known brands that have a strong following plus an incentive-driven loyalty program.

- *Monopoly*
  If your hotel is the only hotel in a specific location, it will have a monopoly where guests have minimal alternatives but to use your hotel. These locations included within the grounds of an airport or a casino or a medical precinct where a medi-hotel provides specialised services to patients.

## Cons in hotels and resorts

Hospitality accommodation carries significant risk and should only be undertaken if the feasibility is positive and careful researched. The following are the main factors that could inhibit new developments:

- *Trading volatility*
  Cash-flows are volatile as they rely heavily on the day to day guest arrivals. Occupation levels could be affected due to seasonal changes, the general economy or an external shock such as pilot strikes. This volatility is aggravated using management agreements as opposed to leases, which are commonly used in the industry.

- *Return not in line with the risk*
  Hotel and resort developments are riskier than other real estate due to their business element. Despite this inherent risk profile, this asset class has traded at initial yields on par with office yields.

- *Operator and owner alignment of objectives*
  The interests of operators and owners are not aligned. The operator's business depends on the quality and state of the property. Still, the owner wants to maximise investment returns and minimise outgoings.

- *Exit strategy*
  A developer's exit strategy is limited as they would be required to hold and operate the development for at least three years to maximise their investment.

- *Alignment of industry*
  The success of a hotel or resort development is highly dependent on other sectors such as airlines, tour operators and tourism marketing bodies. These matters are generally not in control by the operators.

- *Difficult to finance*
  Due to trading volatility, most hotels are difficult to secure funding from lenders. Most operators prefer to offer a management agreement which means that if trading is low, it is not their responsibility. If a lease can be secured with the operator, the banks will look at the financing more seriously.

- *Labour intensive*
  The hospitality accommodation industry requires a numerous, qualified and increasingly costly workforce, which is often unused during the long low season periods.

## Tips in developing hotels and resorts

- *Branding is important*
  Developing a hotel or resort without a well-known brand will require significant capital and time to market a new development. Secondly, branded hotels and resorts can provide valuable input into the planning and design, marketing and operations.

- *Be selective of the brand*
  If you have found an ideal location for a new hotel or resort, do not select one specific brand only. Offer the opportunity to several brands and let them compete to be the operator. It will place you in a better position to negotiate an advantageous management contract.

- *Try and avoid a management agreement.*
  As mentioned, hotels and resorts are exceedingly difficult to finance, and most lenders will not provide development funding if the contract with an operator is a management agreement only. They would like to see a healthy level of income in the initial years of operation, such as a lease agreement. If the

operator is not prepared to provide a lease, then ask them to give a minimal annual guaranteed income for the first three years.

- *Do not let fantasy and emotions determine your project*
  When travelling overseas, one can easily get inspired by the design of a hotel or resort that is exceptional in design. While it is essential to create something unique to the market, one should always ask if this will be accepted in the local market.

## Conclusion

The developments types outlined in this chapter only provides a broad overview, so it will be vital that one should do more research before developing any one of them. Similarly, while the development types explained under the earlier chapters provided more information, they too will require additional reading or research. Remember, each asset class has its nuances and peculiarities that make them successful. Therefore, an in-depth study should be undertaken so that you have full knowledge of the asset class as this will provide you with confidence before committing to one of these developments.

# Chapter 18

# CONCLUSION

After reading this book, you have probably concluded that real estate development is a risky business! But if it is planned and managed correctly, the rewards can be immense. Real estate development has the potential for personal satisfaction and can be both financially rewarding and intellectually stimulating. When a development is completed, and the buildings occupied, the developer can stand back and look at the fruits of their labour. This satisfaction is even greater when the project becomes a financial success.

## Plan your strategy

Before starting your first or next development, it is essential that you formulate an effective business strategy. As I have mentioned several times, there have been countless financial disasters in property development because of bad planning. Conversely, there have been as many stories of success which has come as a result of sound business planning principles. If you follow this lead, you could become a member of this group.

Treat your approach to a real estate development strategy as though you are starting a new business. All modern businesses require a well-constructed business plan setting out a strategy for the next three to five years. Such a plan must include your goals, both long- and short-term, a description of the type or category of development you intend tackling and the market opportunities you have anticipated for it. Also, outline the resources and means you will employ to achieve your goals in the case of a downturn in the property market. Your plan should allow for a certain amount of flexibility and be reviewed every year or at the completion of a project and adjusted where you deem fit or according to any changes that may have occurred.

## Focus on timing

In Chapter 5, I cited that timing within the real estate cycle is a critical factor in real estate development. To realise correct timing, you must be patient and extremely analytical with each development. Do not be pushed or influenced by consultants or agents who may have a different agenda to your own or who may have a different perception of the current and future market. Do your research and make your own value judgement.

Another suggestion is to avoid your emotions getting the better of you when hearing news of other developers making fortunes on their projects. These developers will have planned their schemes several months or years beforehand and are now selling at the peak of a boom. Avoid having 'herd mentality', as you may be too late to catch the peak and, like the rest of the herd and lose a great deal of your hard-earned money which may even push you to bankruptcy.

## Focus on location

In real estate circles, the word location is part of the daily vocabulary. Although timing has been expressed as an essential factor, location is equally important. If you have missed the current economic cycle boom and have enough funds to sustain holding costs, a well-located property will either return the capital you invested or make a good profit at the next peak.

Many small but successful developers focus their real estate interests within a specific radius from their home or business. By concentrating in a particular area, you will gain expert knowledge of the local conditions, such as the market, present and future prices, community trends and attitudes and, more importantly, the best location for the type of project you are developing. Even a simple decision to buy a block of land on the wrong side of the road could determine the success or failure of the development.

## Focus on a specific type of development

In starting as a developer, you should evaluate which type of real estate development is best suited to your personality, financial position and, importantly, what will interest and motivate you. As seen in the preceding chapters, there are three broad areas of development, namely, residential, commercial and special purpose that are in turn broken into subcategories. After selecting the type of development, you are interested in, investigate the intricacies of the subject development. By becoming an expert in a specific area, you should, after some time, automatically be able to gauge a good development from a bad one. It increases your likelihood of success.

## Set the correct finance structure

The financial structure of a development project could be the fine line between success and failure. In good times interest rates are low, and markets are buoyant, but this could turn around in a matter of months and jeopardise the financial position of your existing or committed development. When analysing your feasibility study, test the sensitivity of your figures, such as:

- What if the interest rates increased by three to five per cent during the project?
- What if you cannot sell the development as planned?
- What if you cannot find tenants before the completion of the project?
- What if you lost your job?
- What if there is a dispute with the builder or the builder liquidates during the construction?

There are several other "what ifs" and you should have a financial solution to each of these possible problems. Make sure that you have enough access to additional finances should the worst occur.

## Gain knowledge

They say that knowledge is power, and power is financial security. You do not need an excellent academic career or a university degree to be a successful real estate developer. Many wealthy developers in Australia had little formal education, and many of them are immigrants who could not speak a word of English before they arrived here. But they all followed the same course of action, and that was to gain as much knowledge as they could about real estate. To obtain that knowledge, you do not necessarily have to go back to school or take additional educational courses, although this would help. One should to speak to and ask many questions of experts in the industry, and networking and attending seminars can achieve this. Another source of knowledge is to read books or take a course on real estate. Your local library will have a section of books covering this subject, and there are many courses now offered on the internet. But the most important way of gaining knowledge is through experience. It means starting a project and learning from it. Start with a small project before venturing on to the more complex and lucrative developments.

## Set your goals

Set your goals and follow your dream. On the bookshelves, in seminars and on talk shows, we often hear motivational speakers advocate the principles of goal setting. These same principles apply in the real estate development game, but you must remember to have goals that are realistic and flexible. We all dream of becoming millionaires overnight, and while this is possible with a single development, it will probably not happen with your first project; it will take quite a few years of trial and error. So, when setting your goals, target your ultimate dream but then break it up into smaller, realistic, attainable goals. With real estate development being cyclical, your goals will have to change according to the conditions that prevail at the time, but this should not divert from your ultimate dream; it is a matter of formulating another strategy to reach your target.

## Enjoy the journey

Real estate development can be compared to a rollercoaster ride. There will be many ups and downs, but at the same time, it is stimulating. It is a risky business, but the rewards can be immense if you develop cautiously. Although anything can change without warning, be prepared to take some risks and learn from the experience. If you are an overcautious person and a pessimist, this business is not for you, as you will be too afraid to take that first step to enrich yourself both mentally and financially. But if you have money available and some knowledge of real estate and are prepared to tolerate an occasional attack of nerves, then tackle a single home project. Do your homework and be cautious and you will sleep well at night knowing that your money can appreciate faster than many other investments or businesses.

www.ingramcontent.com/pod-product-compliance
Lightning Source LLC
Chambersburg PA
CBHW031808190326
41518CB00006B/246